Tips for Recording Musicians

John Harris

PC Publishing

PC Publishing
Export House
130 Vale Road
Tonbridge
Kent TN9 1SP
UK

Tel 01732 770893
Fax 01732 770268
email pcp@cix.compulink.co.uk

First published 1995

© PC Publishing

ISBN 1 870775 37 6

British Library Cataloguing in Publication Data

A catalogue record for this book is available from the British Library

Printed and bound in Great Britain by Bell & Bain, Glasgow

Tips for Recording Musicians

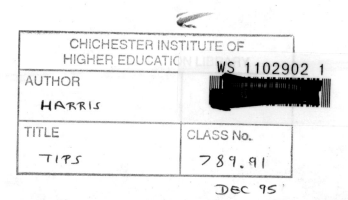

Dedication
To Jude

Contents

Introduction
1 The right tools for the job, 1
2 Getting the best results from your desk, 11
3 Arranging and overdubbing, 20
4 Recording acoustic instruments, 30
5 Some useful effects for acoustic instruments, 38
6 Recording electric guitars, 41
7 Production effects for electric guitars, 49
8 Recording drums, 54
9 Drum production techniques and effects, 64
10 Vocals – recording and production techniques, 67
11 Effects for vocals, 76
12 MIDI in the studio, 80
13 How do I get a good mix? 94
14 Post production tips, 106
Technospeak explained, 114
Index, 119

Foreword

I have known John Harris for more years than either of us care to remember and we've worked together on many projects. John's skill as an engineer has never been in question, but what really impresses me most is the way that he can work with the most awkward of musicians without giving any outward signs that he would like to kill them! Like many of us, John got into recording via being a musician, and aside from being a very accomplished guitarist, John has also played flute, mandolin, keyboards, and now he's well on his way to becoming a serious harp player. The latter may seem an odd choice, but you have to keep in mind his Welsh origins!

Over the years, John has worked in a number of studios, from the most rudimentary home setup to some fairly heavyweight pro setups, and I think he'd agree with me that most of what you learn about recording comes from having to make do with a system that has limitations. In the days when 4-track recording was all you could ever hope to aspire to, we had to pay a lot more attention to things like levels, gain structure and balance than we do now, because it was invariably necessary to mix several instruments, plus their effects, to each track. And of course, we are both pre-MIDI, though we succumbed to its lure as soon as we could afford our first Ataris!

In this book, John has not only compiled an enormous wealth of practical information on all aspects of recording, mixing and music production, he's also managed to keep it refreshingly concise – something he doesn't always do when he's being paid by the word for magazine articles! No doubt his experience in writing for magazines such as *Sound on Sound* has helped hone his literary skills as well as his musical ones, and I feel this book will be of enormous value to anyone involved in home recording, regardless of their existing level of knowledge. After all, even if you only learn one really useful new thing from a book, you're already got your money's worth, but in the case of this book, I'm sure you'll learn a lot more than that. I can hardly wait for my free copy!

Paul White, Editor *Sound On Sound* magazine

1 The right tools for the job

You may well be reading this section after you've spent your hard earned cash buying gear, but don't treat it as a redundant chapter – there's still a lot you can pick up if you intend to upgrade in the future.

❏ Your budget

Be realistic, we all want to get the best that we can afford, but don't forget the added extras when you're getting a list together. Plugs and cable are often missed when buying a multitrack and desk, and are you going to need patchbays and a longer multicore too? And for the MIDI musician there are also things like the interface, tape synchroniser and MIDI peripherals to consider.

❏ Buying the stuff

In an ideal world every salesman would try to be helpful and tailor a system to your exact needs, but more realistically they will try and sell you the gear they have in stock. Although items can be ordered, you could have to wait some time if they're being imported from America or Japan. Obviously ring round for quotes but larger discounts are often to be had by buying from one retailer. Once you've established what you really want get a written quote and see what you can really afford!

Finally I hate to mention it but the dreaded VAT can increase the bill by hundreds of pounds, so you need to know exactly what you need to do the job whether you're buying a portastudio or a digital audio editor – there's little room for gear that can't earn its keep.

❏ The essentials

Your shopping list obviously depends on the type of music you intend to record as well as your budget. Every studio needs a desk of some sort, a monitor system, a two track and some effects, but for instrumental and dance music a tape based multitrack recorder may not be essential.

❑ The tapeless studio

Tapeless recording and the sequencer

The tapeless studio is based around the sequencer for recording and data manipulation, and therefore the more powerful it is the better. Advantages over workstation-based sequencers include on-screen editing, larger memory, faster processing speed, software updates and many functions applicable to the studio – like MIDI control of the mix itself. Quite a number of keyboards have a basic sequencer built in and are adequate for small compositions, but they have limited note storage capacity and can manipulate the data on small screen only.

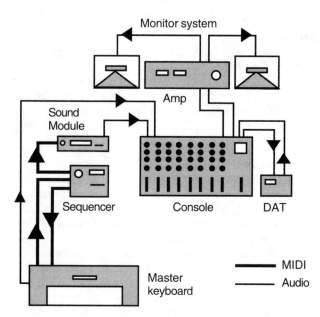

The tapeless studio – a typical setup

Hard disk recording

The market is orientated towards software which combines MIDI sequencing and hard disk recording in one working environment. The data manipulation currently available to MIDI recording, such as cut and paste, quantisation, editing and mixing, can therefore be applied to analogue instruments like guitars and drums once they have been recorded.

Currently they are prohibitively expensive (one stereo minute of recording requires around 10 megabytes of HD storage), but this is undoubtedly the future for tapeless recording. It is worth checking out the potential of a computer as digital recorder if you choose one for sequencing.

Desk format

Many sound modules have separate outputs, but, to take advantage of this individual sound control potential to change the equalisation or add effects to a specific channel, a minimum format of 12 – 2 is necessary. This shorthand actually means that you can route twelve individual channel signals to two output faders (left and right) for stereo mixdown. You don't need a desk with subgrouping and monitor channels unless you intend to include a multitrack at some point, but the more line inputs the better.

EQ

You will need a desk with some EQ but this need only be basic high frequency and low frequency control because many of the sound modules need only rudimentary equalisation work. For more creative uses of EQ a mid frequency control would be useful, but remember that you can equalise the sounds in synthesisers and samplers by using the filters.

Effects sends

Two effects sends and four or more dedicated effects returns (remember your effects outputs are usually stereo) plus insert points on every channel are minimum requirements. And at least two channels with microphone inputs would be useful if you're going to do any sampling. For dance, two RIAA inputs for turntables are helpful to match the level to the desk.

MIDI muting

Many people assume that because you can mute your sound modules via MIDI then there will be no noise on the corresponding desk channel. Not so, the channel electronics will still be there insidiously hissing away in the background. For one channel you're not going to notice but for more the noise will build up. MIDI muting on the desk controlled from your sequencer could therefore be useful if your music has a lot of quiet sections that you wish to remain quiet by closing down the unused channels.

3

The advantages of tapeless recording

Superb sound quality as the sounds are being recorded first generation to the two track master, low tape costs – multitrack tape is pretty expensive although you do have to bear the smaller cost of DAT and normal cassettes so it's not quite a tapeless studio for most! In addition there's the ease with which data can be manipulated, saved and recalled.

❏ Multitrack tape recording

The Portastudio

Desk and tape machine are combined within the small chassis of the portastudio making it ideal, where space is at a premium, or as a portable recording notebook. A higher tape speed and good quality cassettes yield the best results, and some form of noise reduction is essential with such a narrow tape width.

Useful features of a portable multitrack

The more channels the better as you will inevitably use more as you start building up the system. Simple monitor channels and at least one dedicated effect send/return are vital. Insert points and line outputs on every channel are helpful, particularly if you intend to submix the portastudio to a larger desk in the future. As for equalisation, most come with the bare essentials, but the more sophisticated will have a sweep mid in addition to the basic high and low frequency controls.

How many tracks do I need?

Dance music is based around sequenced parts and so there is not much analogue material needed. A four track would be perfectly adequate for recording just lead and backing vocals when they are not being sampled, remembering that one track would have to be given up to tape synchronisation code. An eight track would leave the options open for adding more real instrumentation like guitars and percussion and even recording delay and reverb effects if you are short of outboard for the mix.

Recording bands

For a band with real drums, eight track is the minimum to produce a good demo, although you can obtain decent results from a four track with care. The disadvantage of the latter is the compromised drum sound, heavily submixed and often in mono. Amazing things have been done with the portastudio, witness the ten track bounce, but remember that every time you bounce down you are losing a little quality and clarity.

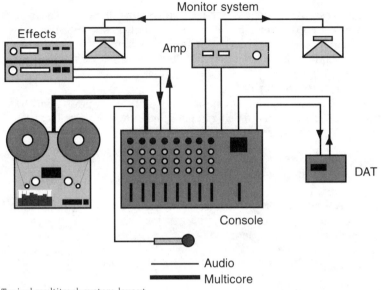

Typical multitrack system layout

Synchronisation

An eight or sixteen track machine with a sequencer synchronised to it can yield excellent results, but a sixteen track gives you more options when your music is based around acoustic instruments.

For example you can have more than one take and then choose the best bits. The capacity to layer sounds and thus build up a good production sound is better too, and for many the choice is between an eight track with sequencer, or a sixteen track. Naturally everyone wants both, but, for cases where this is not possible, a band or small studio would get more out of a sixteen track than an eight, whereas the one or two person operation would benefit from an eight track machine plus sequencer.

Noise reduction

Only a consideration when you're buying an analogue machine, there are three types available – dbx, Dolby C and Dolby S. The last is the most transparent and naturally the most expensive, but dbx and Dolby C are perfectly adequate systems. You can switch them out, but for narrow track formats of less than half inch the noise level is unacceptable.

Side effects of noise reduction are most noticeable with dbx where record errors like drop out may be magnified by the 'compansion' process, and high record levels can lead to tape saturation and compression with some loss of edge to the sound. It can also have an effect on timecode, which provides a particularly nasty sort of sound for tape machines to deal with. Fortunately most multitracks have an option to switch the noise reduction off for the timecode track!

Analogue or digital?

SVHS tape based digital machines are still a cheaper option than HD recording systems and are being bought for serious projects by home recordists and small studio owners.

Digital pros
> No noise reduction, audible print through, wow, flutter, or audible noise floor
> Options for MIDI control and timecode without giving up a track
> Accurate tape counter
> Digital back up and track transfer between machines
> Cheaper tape cost, particularly as you increase tracks

Digital cons
> Expense.
> Some digital format incompatibilities between machines
> No desired compression and tape saturation effects possible
> Has to be transferred for accurate and swift editing
> Varispeed limited on budget machines
> Can't reverse tape

The desk – split vs. in-line

With monitor channels that are laid out on the same strip as the main channels, the in-line desk will always suit the more compact and bijou premises because of its smaller physical size. The split console however offers more dedicated features like equalisation and auxiliary sends which have to be shared with the main channel on an in-line desk. Yet the main distinction between the two designs is how the signal is routed to tape.

The in-line signal path goes directly from the channel fader bus to the tape machine whereas the split console imposes an extra gain section by sending the signal via the sub group fader.

In the interests of flexibility the whole concept has been improved by the appearance of the hybrid desk which allows you to use either method by adding a small sub group fader section.

The advantages of this system are threefold. First, it's easy to combine channel signals and send them to a single track on the tape machine via the sub group fader. Second, you can use the subgroup faders on mixdown by assigning them to the left right bus and routing a whole drum kit for example to a stereo pair. Thirdly it easily accommodates those who are used to the split console approach.

How many channels?
You always seem to need more channels than you have so my advice is to get a desk that has double the amount of channels as tracks on your tape machine. This also leaves you with a desk that is usable if you upgrade the tape machine. Furthermore desk design changed with the advent of MIDI and now any self respecting console will convert monitor channels to line inputs at the push of a button, instantly doubling the channels you have available for mixdown. Extra channels for effects returns are always useful.

Desk shorthand
Let's say for example a desk is described as a 16-8-2. This is almost self explanatory:

16	8	2
Channels	subgroups	stereo

But what about the desks where the monitor channels are used as extra line inputs? You may see these advertised as 16 – 8 – 16 – 2:

16	8	16	2
Channels	subgroups	monitor channels	stereo

Effects returns can also be included in the numbers when for example a 16 – 8 – 16 – 2 desk with four stereo returns claims 40 channel mixdown capability.

Equalisation
The minimum you need for recording bands is two fixed shelving frequencies for HF and LF control with a sweep mid. Two sweep mids are preferable, especially when dealing with drums, but, as it's the kick drum that requires most attention, an outboard EQ patched in to the channel may be of more use.

Auxiliary sends and inserts
The ability to have stereo foldback is useful, so two pre fade and two post fade sends are the minimum requirement. Look for switchable pre/post fade sends for flexibility on mixdown.

Insert points are sometimes labelled auxiliary sends too which is confusing as they are channel specific. Make sure that they are also on the master channels and if possible the subgroups. They are rarely found on the monitor channels and effect returns on budget desks.

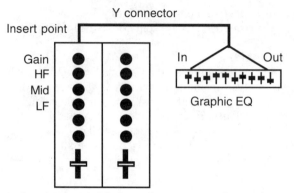

Outboard EQ can aid desk EQ where more specific sound control is required

Others

Direct outputs on split consoles, two track returns, channel mutes and simple effect returns are all likely to be found on a budget console. More rare are EQ on/off, solo in place, high pass filters, left/right to cue mix, a talkback microphone and MIDI muting And what about effects?

❑ Compression

Even the tapeless studio will benefit from having a compressor when some extra punch is needed for a sound, or even to run a vocal through before it goes to a sampler. A stereo compressor is the best option because you can link it across a stereo mix or use it as two individual mono units. In addition to dealing with poor dynamics it can be used as a creative production tool. Many compressors now also come with added extras like expander gates, enhancers and frequency filters, which can be used independently of compression and thus save you having to buy an extra dedicated unit.

❑ Reverb and delay

Some form of multi-effects unit with a decent reverb is necessary to give that professional quality to the mix and an opportunity for creative sound manipulation using other patches. You can cover most of the things you need to do on a mix with two effects units. Look for complementary ones from different manufacturers. Older delay effects and preset reverbs can also be picked up secondhand quite cheaply now, and there's always a use for these when the multi-effects unit is tied up on the mix.

❑ Gates

Dedicated noise gates are useful but not essential. Used to isolate individual drums and deal with noisy guitars they can cut out spill and the dreaded amp hiss and hum. As a creative tool they are excellent but rather a luxury in the small recording system.

❑ Enhancers

These are useful for dealing with recordings made on equipment with a compromised bandwidth, but if you've got a tight budget it's better left to the post production stage where they can be hired or borrowed. For individual sounds they can be very useful to pep up a sound lacking in HF provided you don't overdo it. Not essential.

❑ Microphones

It's worth having at least one good microphone in the studio which you will then undoubtedly end up using for most of the work. On a small budget a good brand name dynamic such as the Shure SM 58 is fine, but if you can afford it a good quality capacitor/electret will lend the professional touch to your recordings.

❑ Quick guide to mics

Dynamics for vocals, louder sounds like drums, electric guitar and bass guitar.

Capacitor mics and electrets for vocals, low level acoustic instruments, high frequency sounds like cymbals and hi hats.

Tandy pressure zone microphones (PZM) are good value for money and therefore extremely popular in small studios. Replace the jack with a male XLR to improve their operating level. They may also be converted to phantom power. Use for live recording, instruments with HF content, live room.

Individually miking a drum kit requires lots of microphones, stands and leads, but there are simpler ways to mic up a kit for which you will still need at least two good microphones.

❑ Monitor system

The most common question is whether the hi-fi will be good enough for monitoring. Studio requirements are different from domestic ones in that a flat frequency response is required to evaluate sound sources. Speakers lacking in bass or flattering in the treble department will affect the way you record and mix, and amplifier equalisation should also be avoided. Levels too are in question as it's quite easy to drive a domestic amplifier into distortion and damage your speakers when dealing with loud sound sources like drums. The acid test is whether the mixes you do on your hi-fi sound good on a variety of systems.

❏ Level matching

Is not the problem it used to be as equipment is generally designed for the dual operating levels required by studio and live performance. When buying microphones, remember that studio equipment is low impedance (most small PA amps now offer low as well as high impedance inputs). Don't forget that you will have to lower the output levels on effects when you plug them into a backline amp by around −20dB, that passive electric guitars and bass guitars will need to be impedance matched to a desk input using a DI box, and multiple headphones need to operate around the same impedance to avoid level differences.

❏ Buying secondhand

Unless you are making a considerable saving by buying secondhand it's not worth losing out on guarantee and back up facilities. However, equipment can easily be checked for problems and it is fairly simple to tell if gear has had a hard life by the condition it's in. The most obvious faults usually involve noise of some kind – strange clicks, buzz, distortion, crackle or a processing disorder, and you should establish that all the connections are in order.

Analogue tape machines are more difficult to check, and a responsible owner will have had the machine serviced before selling it on. Heads with excessive wear look flat and worn and are expensive to replace. Check the levels with a 1kHz tone and the treble reproduction with 10kHz, listening for treble loss and warble.

Digital tape machines like the Alesis ADAT have a function which allows you to see the total running time of the drum motor by using the set, locate and stop buttons.

2 Getting the best results from your desk

❏ Desk design

Budget desk design has changed enormously for the better since I first started recording, and it's really been in the physical size, amount of channels and facilities that the improvements are most marked.

The size has actually got smaller and therefore more manageable for the home and small semi pro studio, the advent of tape synchronisation brought a demand for previously redundant monitor channels to become available as line inputs on mixdown for MIDI triggered sounds, and facilities like solo in place and a degree of automation, previously only the province of the larger consoles, are now almost fitted as standard.

Step up the ladder to the desks designed for the small pro studio and we find consoles which are more often than not also found in the pre-production rooms of large pro studios. The fact that they are built to stand up to the rigorous testing of people at the top of their profession speaks for itself, and you are likely to see these desks in the home set ups of recording artists and producers as well as the professional small studio.

What inevitably differentiates the larger desks from their smaller brethren is the quality of the components, and it is in the arena of noise and sonic integrity that you have to work the hardest if you want to get a really good sound from budget equipment.

❏ Noise limitation

Nearly all equipment conspires to produce noise, and this is most audible when you run gain stages flat out. One of the main problems with budget equipment is that this noise is noticeable when you're dealing with music that is dynamically more low key than full tilt rock and pop.

In the latter the ratio of signal level to noise is usually so high that you can only hear it at the start and end of tracks where it can be edited out. For the former the more you become accustomed to the desk the more you will begin to notice and struggle with noise when working with acoustic instruments and recording quiet or sparse tracks.

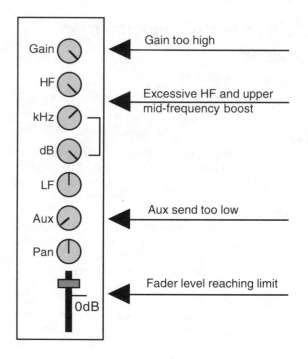

Potential sources of noise in your desk

Signal to noise figures are given for desks but these are indecipherable to most and usually treated as optimistic by those who understand them. So without the aid of measuring equipment how do you determine at the outset where the limits are on your desk?

Well the answer is that you are equipped with measuring equipment – your ears, and you can be thoroughly pragmatic about your methods. The project outlined below for input gain should be followed through with the monitors at a fairly high level – so be absolutely sure that no signal is going to suddenly come through the desk and damage them. It could also be done with headphones which will provide a more critical listening test, but once again make sure that no loud signal will suddenly appear – those ears are precious!

○ *PROJECT*

Establishing the optimum gain level before noise

Input gain – With the monitor level turned up, the channel fader at 0dB, EQ switched out and the channel routed to the left/right faders (also set at 0dB), gradually increase the input gain and make a note of where it starts to become noisy. If your desk has a mic/line switch then remember that these will be working at different operating levels, but if the gain pot is the same – normally the case on a budget console, the last quarter turn of the gain pot's movement should start bringing up the hiss.

You are now aware of the point where the input gain begins adding noise and can therefore judge whether it's worth pushing the gain past that point when a signal is present. If the signal itself is noisy then this will of course worsen the overall S/N ratio.

Running any gain stage too high will introduce noise, so pay attention particularly to HF and upper mid EQ boost, effects send/returns, channel, sub group and master faders.

❑ Dealing with low level signals – line input

Symptom Loss of treble and low level.
Solution Impedance mismatch. Are you running a high impedance output for example an electric guitar with passive pickups into the low impedance input of a desk? If so use a DI box or matching transformer.
Symptom Low line level output from sound module.
Solution Check mix level of sound within module and MIDI trigger velocity value if using a sequencer. If these are fine then use a pre-amp or DI box.

❑ Dealing with low level signals – mic input

Symptom Low level of signal.
Solution Check microphone lead (turn monitors to low level before unplugging anything), change the microphone for a more sensitive model with higher output, or move the mic closer to the sound source provided it doesn't compromise the sound, or get the musician to play with heavier dynamic if possible.

❑ Faders

The fader is also a gain stage and as such it can also be noisy when run at high levels. Typically once you start getting above +5dB you could start to notice noise, and if you are running all your channels at that level then you can expect that noise to be multiplied! Remember too that your main left/right and sub group outputs use faders and these shouldn't end up at a high level because your signal matching is poor somewhere back down the line.

❏ Other sources of noise
Symptom Your effects returns are noisy.
Solution
(a)You have a level mismatch between the desk and the effects unit. Check the operating levels of desk aux sends and returns, and make sure that the effects unit matches them. Most operate at 0 to +4dB. This means that guitar pedal effects unless specified are not going to work well on a desk aux send.
(b)You are not driving the input level of the effects unit hard enough and are turning up the level of the aux return and effect output to compensate.
(c) You are using a particularly noisy patch like a flanger and may have to trim the HF equalisation by a few dBs.
(d) If your desk has MIDI muting then mute the aux returns when they are not being used.

❏ Ground loops
Although some budget equipment produces a background level of noise, ground loop hum is constant and audible as soon as the offending equipment is plugged in. This makes the perpetrator easier to trace if you build up a system piece by piece. It is best dealt with by the well documented method of running a 100 ohm resistor in series with the screen of an unbalanced cable at one end, connecting the screen to the jack underneath the jack cover. You may have dealt with it already by removing the mains earth but this is not a safe option.

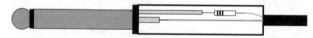

Connecting a 100 ohm resistor in series with the screen often cures hum

❏ Radiated hum and interference
Can usually be dealt with by moving a piece of equipment or cable and can be caused by:

Cables running parallel to mains or alongside transformers.
External power supplies in proximity to each other or near cables.
Position of equipment in a rack.
Guitar pickups (particularly single coil) from equipment racks, computer screens, fluorescent lights and dimmers.

❏ Open channel noise

Try leaving the monitor level up and gradually routing channels to the left/right bus with all the faders turned down and listen. The simple act of routing to the left/right bus and leaving an effect send open adds a small amount of hiss which can have a cumulative effect on unused channels. De-selecting unused channels and making sure that input gains and EQ are out is good practice.

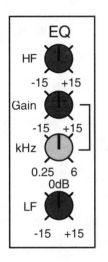

Standard desk EQ with shelving HF and LF
and swept mid controls

❏ Using equalisation

To equalise or not to equalise? Engineers have varying opinions on the subject which are summarised in the next few sections.

❏ Getting the right sound at source

Basically you make sure that the sound from the instrument is the one that you want to hear and don't use equalisation. Take the example of an electric guitar. Different pickup selections, plectrum sizes, playing attack, playing position between neck and bridge and string condition all combine to make up the sound – and that's before you even consider the options on the amplifier and the microphone type and position! Let's say that the sound requires more treble – rather than turn up the HF on the desk EQ. you would try another pickup, a different microphone position or maybe even a different guitar.

❑ Equalising at mixdown

There is also a case for getting the sound as good as you can and not committing any EQ to tape, but leaving your options open for the mixdown stage where a slight tweak might be enough to sit the sound in the mix.

❑ Remedial equalisation

As I know very well from experience, not everyone has the luxury of time to experiment when dealing with a poor sound source. Bands on a tight budget are always watching the clock, and the instrument you want to record may be the only one you can lay your hands on. This means that you have to resort to equalisation in an attempt to fix the sound.

Let's take as an example a drum kit with old drum heads. You can't just send the drummer out to buy a new set if there's no money to pay for it so you have to make do by seriously boosting the upper mid EQ frequencies in an attempt to put back the presence that the old drum skins have lost. Naturally once you do so the level of noise being generated by the equalisation going to tape – most audible in the upper mid and high frequency range – is increased, and you're also losing the natural sound of the kit. Fortunately for a loud band the hiss will be obscured, but if you're attempting anything subtle you will ultimately have to deal with a noisy mix.

Another example would be at mixdown where you have to alter a sound heavily to make it fit with the others. Really you're trying to compensate for not getting the sound right in the first place.

❑ Creative equalisation

So far I've been putting the case for getting a sound without having to do much EQ work, but that doesn't mean you can't use the equalisation at all to creatively alter a sound before you commit it to tape. Take the telephone voice, cutting the bass and treble and boosting the upper mid will get you the sound, and that's pretty extreme equalisation work. Yet there's no reason why you can't apply extremes to musical sounds too – never be afraid to experiment.

❑ Getting used to your EQ

All that's very well but what is your own desk capable of? Most budget desk EQ consists of a high frequency, low frequency and sweep mid section. If you're lucky you'll have two sweep mids but parametric equalisation is out because it's far too expensive. Your swept mids may be called semi parametric or quasi parametric but they're missing the all important bandwidth control (Q) which makes them truly so. Instead they have two out of the three controls – gain and frequency.

○ PROJECT

Check out your EQ

To get used to what these and your shelving HF and LF do, try running a simple drum machine pattern with kick drum, snare and hi-hats through the channel.

1. Turn up the HF gain then turn it down to a negative dB position before returning it to 0dB. Notice that it is the hi-hats which are most affected because they have the most energy in this region. Also on turning up the HF the kick drum will get more attack because it has some harmonics that make up the attack portion of its sound in this area. However it will not increase in level as the hi-hat does because there is not much sound energy in the kick drum to boost at this frequency. The snare meanwhile will have the actual sound of the snares and the crispness increased but again will not increase in level in the same way that the hi-hat does. All will be reversed when the gain is in the negative position.

2. Repeat the above using the LF control. This time the kick drum is greatly affected, the hi-hat not at all and the bass in the snare increased and decreased as you move the control. Notice how weedy the sound is without bass? That's because much of the energy of music is contained in this region.

Another thing you probably observed was that your channel began to overload as you turned up the bass EQ. This is because the EQ gain section is often pre input gain in the signal path. So obviously if you are turning up the EQ gain you may have to trim back the input gain.

3. Using your mid EQ with the gain set to maximum, sweep the frequency control slowly from its lowest to its highest point. Notice how different harmonics are emphasised in the sounds. In the lower range the snare and kick drum are altered producing a hard, mid quality quite typical of the 200 – 600Hz range, but once above this the attack of both kick and snare come to the fore with the hi-hats also being boosted once the range climbs above the 1kHz region.

4. Try the sweep exercise once again only this time with the gain at its minimum setting.

What you should have learned from this project is that different sounds have more sound energy in one frequency band than another (although they do overlap), that high frequency energy can mask noise (try turning up the HF control to maximum without any hi-hat in the mix!), that you can overload a channel with too much boost, and finally that you can manipulate the sound by using boost or cut on the sweep mids.

❏ Additive and subtractive EQ

Cutting the EQ gain is subtractive and a more subtle method of dealing with sounds, but subjectively there are differences between the two methods and your ears must judge.

○ PROJECT

Adding attack to a kick drum

Compare:

Additive: Boost at 2 – 4kHz emphasises upper mid frequency attack portion of sound.

Subtractive: Cut at 200 – 300 Hz makes upper mid frequencies and bass seem more prominent to emphasise the attack.

❏ Using channels – main or monitor channels?

Prioritise the most important sounds to the main channels because they are usually cleaner and have a better gain structure than the monitor channels, in addition to their auxiliary send and EQ benefits. Important effects returns that you want to gain ride, route to tape or equalise quickly are better on main faders.

❏ Running out of channels

Remember that effects returns are simple line inputs and don't have to be used for effects. An insert return on a subgroup fader can be used to get a signal into the desk and the subgroup then routed to the left/right bus for use as a basic channel. This is good for effects returns because a +4dB signal level is usually necessary and most effects have a variable output control.

❏ Submixer

As a final resort a submixer can be connected to two channels of the desk and used for extra inputs like effects returns or a drum mix. See pic opposite.

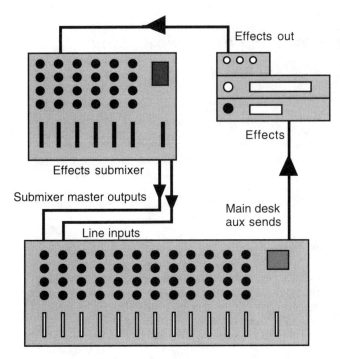

Effects out

Effects

Effects submixer

Submixer master outputs

Line inputs

Main desk
aux sends

Incorporating an effects submixer into the system

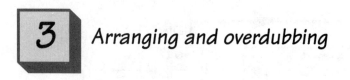

3 Arranging and overdubbing

❏ Pre production

Time spent working on the song before you attempt the master recording is your pre production. This could be as simple as banging out the song idea on a piano or guitar and recording it on a portable recorder or as complex as recording a whole demo using a small multitrack and MIDI system. Everyone has a different way of working – some start with the melody, some with the chords, some with the groove.

Whatever the method this is the time when you should be sorting out the key of the song, the basic chordal construction and the arrangement, with maybe some MIDI programming thrown in. Many professional artists now have a good basic system at home, and work done at this stage with a producer is often transferred to the master recording because something on tape has captured the spirit of the song and is impossible to recreate in different circumstances – the definitive take.

❏ The right key

Whatever your working method the most important thing is to establish the right key. If the singer struggles on the high notes and lacks dynamic control – having to bellow them out or simply be unable to hit the pitch, then the key should be lowered. Yet on occasion singing at the limit of the range can be emotive and powerful.

Two rock examples of this are 'Pride (in the Name of Love)' by U2 and 'Living on a Prayer' by Bon Jovi. Likewise the Black Box mix of 'Ride on Time' was successful because the vocalist was on the edge.

Conversely, if strength is being lost on the low notes, the key needs to be pitched up. If both happen you need to change the melody or have key changes within the song.

So, at this pre production stage it pays to establish the range of a singer unless they already know it (most semi pro singers don't). Once you've committed real instruments to tape you can't change the key easily, and a lot of time can be wasted. One of the joys of working with MIDI at this stage is that you can just hit the transpose key!

○ PROJECT

Finding a singer's vocal range

Sing the lowest note, find that on a keyboard or guitar and progress upwards in semitones to the highest note. Make a note of the highest and lowest notes sung with ease and also observe where the the vocal changes tone within the overall range. It as at these points that you move from one zone to another within that range, and the changeover points can sometimes be weak.

❏ Instrument ranges

Classical musicians have an advantage in their knowledge of the range of instruments, but anyone with a keyboard can experiment with brass, woodwind and string patches to see where they sound good. The advantage of these sounds when voiced on a keyboard is that you can actually play them outside the range too which gives rise to great creative potential. For rock and pop instruments, range charts aren't that readily available, but I've included one in the section on layering sounds later in this chapter.

❏ Some standard song arrangements

I personally don't believe that a song should have to fit into a pigeon hole in terms of either arrangement or length, but it can't have escaped your attention that pop songs have developed a formulaic style of writing over the past thirty years. Yet you can be inventive within the format and what follows are a few ideas you can start with. Notice that I'm using a musical shorthand of an upright stroke for each bar | with a tilted one / after every group of four.

This is a standard shorthand with which you can fit an entire song arrangement onto a scrap of paper, back of a cigarette packet or whatever's to hand. Full score and chord charts take up too much space and a lot of people can't read music. The only prerequisite for the shorthand is that you can count!

❏ Simple pop song

A simple pop song will often run something like this:

Verse 1	IIII/ IIII
Chorus 1	IIII/ IIII
Verse 2	IIII/ IIII
Chorus 2	IIII/ IIII

Middle 8	IIII/ IIII
Rpt. chorus	IIII/ IIII/ IIII/ IIII/ IIII etc.
to fade.	

It even looks pretty uninspiring on paper doesn't it? Try spicing it up a bit by changing the length of some of the parts, it may involve re-writing the lyrics but it will be worth it if the song sounds better.

Verse 1	IIII/ IIII/ IIII/ IIII
Chorus 1	IIII/ IIII/
Verse 2	IIII/ IIII
Chorus 2	IIII/IIII/IIII/ IIII
Middle 8	IIII/IIII
Verse 3	IIII/IIII
Ch. to fade	IIII/ IIII/ IIII/ IIII etc.

The second verse is now half the length of the first and gives the song a sense of moving forward with more purpose. The double chorus (chorus 2) should be adding something different for the second half to pick it up while you're still ramming home the hook. Try backing vocals or an additional instrument, possibly playing a counter melody. And while we're on that theme it's also a good idea to introduce a counter melody or extra instrument in verse two to give the sense that the song is building.

Meanwhile at the middle 8 you're ready to take a breather after all this excitement! You could use that old cliche and go for the relative minor chord here. For example if the chorus was in G major (a venerable key for the guitar) it could move in sprightly fashion to Em and easily resolve back to G for the last verse and chorus.

For your grand finale on the repeat choruses you could use the instrumental build up that occurred on chorus 2 and then add some more for the fade out. You may also be tempted by the vile change of key ploy (as used by many artists who should know better when they can't think of anything else to do). This usually ups the key by a tone so if you're in G that means you change to A for the repeat section.

On the cringeworthy but incredibly successful 'I Just called to say I love you' (yuk!), Stevie Wonder actually steps up by a semitone, but even one of my favourite artists, Julian Cope, used the ploy for the hit single 'World Shut Your Mouth'. Psychologically it is designed to lift the song and add excitement. Speaking of which the minor key for the middle 8 tactic has the psychological effect of taking the song to a low so that it can be lifted again by the major key of the chorus. You should never underestimate the psychological power of simple music just because you're a muso!

❑ Take it to the bridge

Running between the verse and the chorus this useful device adds more interest to a boring verse by introducing a new chord sequence and melody, becomes a lead in to a key change for the chorus, or can act as an area of tension before breaking into the chordal resolution and consequent release of the chorus.

You might also think about adding a solo or a short instrumental start, perhaps carrying the theme of the chorus so your arrangement could end up something like this:

Intro	IIII
Verse 1	IIII/ IIII
Bridge	IIII
Chorus 1	IIII/IIII
Instrumental	II
Verse 2	IIII
Bridge	IIII
Chorus 2	IIII/ IIII
Middle 8	IIII/ IIII
Solo	IIII/IIII
Bridge	IIII
Ch to fade...	

Notice how the second verse is shorter and chorus 2 the normal length (otherwise the song will be too long), the solo no more than eight bars (guitarists take note), and the bridge makes a re-appearance to fulfil its pre chorus tension role.

These are just a few suggestions. Of course there are many variations which I suggest you experiment with.

❑ Breaking the mould

You don't have to write a song like this and the above are just tried and tested methods which don't suit quite a lot of musical styles. Dance music has to some extent broken the mould but now has its own cliches – well that's what comes with popularity. If you're looking for something new then I recommend you listen to what's going on at the periphery of the pop, rock, dance and world market for inspiration.

❑ The characteristics of instruments

So you've arranged the song and now you want to start recording the backing. But why do some mixes sound so much better recorded than the rest? The answer is to be found in the choice of instruments, chord voicings and sound layering as much as the actual mixing process. Consider the recording process like painting. You start with an empty canvas and anything you add changes the overall picture so great care is needed at every stage.

❑ Sound envelope

It pays to be aware of the attack, decay, sustain and release character-istics of an instrument (ADSR for short). Take the piano. This has a fast percussive attack, an obvious decay and a sustain and release slope which can be varied using the damper and sustain pedals.

In contrast a violin has a slow attack, the result of drawing a bow across the string to make the string vibrate. Yet a plucked pizzicato or an aggressive string bow can both produce different sounds which are fast in attack and short in duration, despite coming from the same instrument

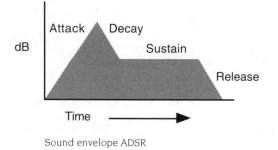

Sound envelope ADSR

Also when emulating an instrument on a synthesiser, be aware of how a real instrumentalist would play. A flautist for example would turn blue and keel over with the sustain a keyboard can muster, and a brass player can play soft legato runs as well as hard, punctuating stabs.

○ PROJECT

Match your songs to your sounds

If you own a sequencer record some phrases with a variety of dynamics and speeds. Loop them and then play them back individually, changing the presets on your sound module on each loop. This will give you a good idea of what suits the sound envelopes of different sounds (Mozart had to do this in his head!).

❑ Mixing sounds

Don't be afraid to try real instruments with synthesised sounds. Analogue synth brass can sound wonderful against the harder tones of real brass, and a small string section can be fleshed out with a string pad. Also when layering synthesised sounds together be aware of their characteristics. For example, a piano layered with strings will retain clarity on a fast run because the percussive piano carries the leading edge of the sound. Replace the strings with a vocal sound and that nimble run will fast become a mess!

❑ Clarity

This is where the real skill of the engineer comes into play, and it's also the area where most demos fall down. Although it's not a craft that can be learned overnight, some basic rules can be applied. A thorough knowledge of where sounds appear in the frequency range is useful yet it's also a case of knowing where the main energy of that sound lies within its frequency range.

❑ Fundamentals and harmonics

All sounds have a fundamental frequency which determines the actual pitch of the note. For example, the open A string on a guitar is actually 110 Hz, and most musicians who have used an automatic tuner will be familiar with the A above middle C at 440 Hz. Yet that's not the end of the story because higher frequency harmonics are also part of that sound when a note is struck.

Take a strummed chord on an acoustic guitar. If all six strings are struck the result is a complex waveform comprising six fundamental notes and their series of harmonics. The strength of these harmonics tends to lessen as they get higher, but many other things – like the instrument's construction, materials and size, string gauge and the velocity of the playing – all influence the resulting sound wave. However the loudest signals are usually the fundamental notes and that's how we perceive the pitch.

It follows then that the open note of A played on the guitar will be more affected by a change of equalisation in the 110 Hz range than one in the 2kHz range because there is more energy in the sound there. However turning up the gain at 2kHz will bring out the presence of the A string by boosting the high frequency harmonics, but for an equal amount of gain increase at both frequencies you should be able to guess which has the most effect!

❏ Sound separation

There is a perfect example of sound separation in the composition of
the drum kit. If we look at the chart we will see why. The kick drum
carries the weighty low frequency end of the kit and sitting above this
the snare and toms occupy a similar range, depending on how they've
been tuned. A clash and resultant lack of clarity is possible between
the snare and the toms, but if you watch a drummer playing you'll
observe that the toms aren't usually hit when the snare is unless it's
the large and low tuned floor tom. The cymbals produce a lot of HF
energy and therefore are well away from the rest of the kit – obviously
the development of the instrument historically has involved the use of
some good listening techniques!

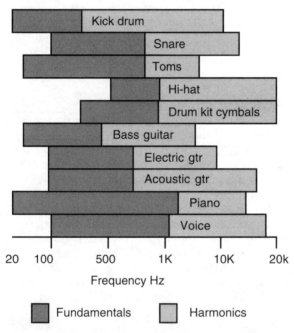

Chart of instrument frequency ranges

○ PROJECT

Sit down and listen!

Listen to one of your favourite songs and try to pick out what
instruments have been used and what makes these particular sounds
fit together.

❏ Making a hole for the vocals

Too many people leave the vocals until last in the overdubbing process but you really need to know two things:

(a) Where they occur so that you don't record major parts where the vocals are meant to be
(b) Where the main frequency strength of the singer lies so that your backing isn't constantly in danger of overpowering the vocals.

To kill two birds with one stone, where tracks are available record a guide vocal and work around that. When this is down you could also try playing with the equalisation on the vocal track to determine where the main frequency energy of the vocalist lies (eventually you will be able to evaluate this by ear). Make sure that the instrument sounds you choose don't conflict with the singer's strong frequency range. When the singing stops you can fill the gap if you need to with a sound of a similar timbre to the voice, but this is by no means essential.

❏ Chord voicings

The choice of a different chord inversion is going to affect not only the instrument's working frequency but it can also help the song dynamically.

Take the case of a band with two guitarists using similar equipment. Unless they're panned hard left and hard right, a way to distinguish one from the other is by altering the chord inversions. While one guitarist thrashes out the chord of A (open position, notes A E A C#) the other could be playing A at the fifth fret, strings 1 – 4 (A C# F A). This will give a more interesting sound texture as well as more clarity.

Another reason to try different inversions is to create tension and a sense of build in an arrangement. Any repeated section in a song will benefit from different chord inversions, and if they are higher it will heighten the tension and excitement of a piece.

○ PROJECT

Swap the chords around

Simple melodies can be improved using different chords underneath. Try taking a melody and trying some out. Substitute chords like the relative minor and sevenths are popular.

❏ Chords to avoid

It's best to avoid chords containing a lot of notes when you are using distortion. If in doubt root and fifth always work best, major thirds are best left out.

Keyboard players especially should be wary of bass chords when playing with a bass guitarist. Again clarity could be a problem unless the sounds chosen have enough separation.

❏ Track sharing

With a limited amount of tracks on your tape machine you inevitably end up having more than one sound per track. You will either have bounced two together and therefore their mix is set, or have one instrument playing when the other is not. In both cases their recorded levels are crucial to achieving a panic-free mix.

When recording the sounds to tape you should listen to the way they interact with what is already there, not just in terms of frequency but level too. A typical scenario could be brass and piano sharing the same track. You may think that if you put them to tape at the same meter level then they will sound the same coming back – this is not the case. The abrasive brass sound with more HF overtones will be louder proving that your ears are what you should trust – just record the sounds to tape at the level you want to hear them in the mix. If the brass needs to be louder than the piano then you can leave it, but if they need to be the same volume you will have to reduce the level to tape of the brass sound.

Some of you may be wondering if this is sound recording practice – what about signal to noise ratio? The simple answer is that if you're using noise reduction on your recordings (which most budget machines have) it can certainly cope with this.

❏ Less is more

When you have only a limited amount of tracks, every sound you record must count. So rather than cram as many mediocre parts as you can onto an eight track by multiple bounces, choose one (at most two) well arranged and played sounds per track. This selective discipline will stand you in good stead for future productions on larger machines and give a far better overall sound to the mix.

Newcomers to recirding often try to fill every space with sound, but gaps can make their own musical statement too!

Finally, remember that you can't mask a bad take by recording more instruments playing in the same place.

❏ A quick note on levels

Certain sounds can trip up the input stages on tape machines and others have obvious side effects for some noise reduction systems. Here's a rough guide:

○ PROJECTS

Analogue, no noise reduction

Record a high level to tape to get the highest S/N ratio. Experiment with the limits of your machine (see also HF note below) and note at what level compression and saturation effects occur.

Analogue with dbx

You can hear the side effects at high levels of compression on drums and some treble loss. Possibility of a slight hiss above bass signals which can't obscure it with HF harmonics.

Sounds with a lot of HF (analogue machines only)

Tape pre-emphasis can boost the recorded HF into tape saturation, fooling the meters so keep the levels down. For example to avoid the familiar 'aerosol' effect, record hi-hats at –7dB.

Digital recording

No tape noise floor but lots of level needed so you're using up all those numbers! Consider using a limiter set at -3dB to get a high level with no overload.

❒ The importance of the monitor mix

None of the above tips would be of any use when sound layering if you are working with a bad monitor mix. First, you would have no idea what levels to record at when track sharing. Second, musicians would find it hard to play to their best ability – could you keep in time to a poor drum mix? Third, chord voicings would be hard to choose if the emphasis was on the wrong instrument – the loudest one, in the mix.

Ideally you should have a good balance on the instruments and be monitoring with some effect like a basic reverb. Often these balances and effects are modified as the overdubbing progresses and you can end up with the song almost ready to mix.

4 Recording acoustic instruments

The influence of world music has dramatically increased the amount of acoustic instruments you may be called upon to record. Each instrument has its own unique sound and this is what makes recording acoustic instruments such a challenge.

❏ Good vibrations

Consider a violin. Like any acoustic instrument it has various parts which vibrate and produce a sound when played – the action of rubbing the bow against the string causes the bridge, body and neck to resonate, the sound waves are amplified by a chamber in which the air is set in vibration and the listener hears a combination of all these plus the effect of room acoustics. Naturally choice and position of the microphone become critical and there is some argument that the best recording of an acoustic instrument would be using stereo microphones at a distance in an acoustically good room. Certainly this is the traditional method, but poor acoustics, the effects of spill in an ensemble situation and choice (you may not want a natural sound) conspire against this for the smaller studio.

❏ Recording in small rooms

If a small room is too live you will find the frequencies emphasised are usually in an unpleasant area of the mid range. So miking an instrument up from a distance in such a room may yield interesting, but not entirely usable results if an even sound is required. However as the tonality of an instrument is stifled by a dead acoustic, you should find that even when close miking in a fairly live area there is a significant improvement to the sound. Try bringing in some reflective material and then experiment with microphone positions.

○ PROJECT

Adjust your room acoustics

To make your acoustics more lively, bring material with a more reflective surface into the playing area, like hardboard or plywood sheets, corrugated metal, even a mirror. Try recording the instrument at various distances away and compare the results.

❏ Choice of microphones

Capacitor and electret microphones are the most widely used for two reasons:

1. Most acoustic instruments produce a fair amount of high frequency detail which these microphones are capable of reproducing.
2. They have a greater sensitivity to the low levels which many acoustic instruments produce and hence can present a workable level to the desk input stage.

This does not rule out dynamic microphones, which are better suited to loud instruments like drums and brass. In fact the best microphones for recording acoustic instruments are those which do not alter the sound artificially, i.e. that have an even frequency response across the audio spectrum. Unfortunately this all means extra expense, and in reality you're usually pushed to afford one of these microphones, let alone a stereo pair! In spite of this you can still achieve good results from the budget microphones I've mentioned elsewhere in the book as long as you are careful with levels and equalisation.

❏ Noise

The level of noise produced by microphones, cables and consoles is a major consideration when recording solo and small ensemble performances where there is nothing to mask it. Hence in exclusively acoustic recordings much emphasis is placed on efficient microphones, quality balanced cabling and careful use of gain structures.

❏ One mic, two, or more?

As you've probably realised by now, a more natural sound will be achieved by stereo miking (after all we have two ears to listen to the original instrument), but the context of the instrument in the rest of the recording is also important. An acoustic guitar mixed in with the other instruments in a band is recorded as a rhythmic texture if it's just strumming along, and the benefits of stereo and natural sound will be lost and inappropriate among the rest of the sounds. As the central focus the opposite is true and stereo miking would certainly improve the listening experience.

In the case of an ensemble playing in a room with good acoustics, stereo microphones are usually placed in the room to capture the overall ambience even when the individual instruments or, in the case of an orchestra, groups of instruments (a string section for example), are miked up.

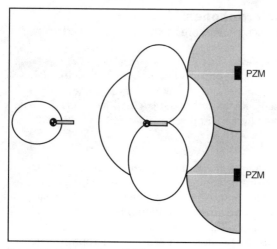

PZM

PZM

If a usable live area is available try a room mic in an omni or figure of eight pattern, or a stereo pair in addition to the close mic.

When using more than one microphone to capture stereo, remember that phase problems will be minimised if they are equidistant from the sound source.

❏ Instruments

In a book of this size it is impossible to cover microphone placement and techniques for all the instruments, so I have picked out those which you are most likely to encounter. If a usable live area is available you should assume that room mics in an omni or figure of eight polarity should be tried in addition to close miking, using unidirectional and wide cardioid response patterns. Naturally try different microphone positions and treat the ones suggested as a starting point.

○ PROJECT

Using headphones

A useful technique for recording acoustic instruments is to wear headphones and send the microphone signal to them on the foldback. As the player plays and you move the microphone you can clearly hear tonal variation, check for phase cancellation and make a decision on microphone placement without having to run back and forth to the control room to listen over the monitors.

❏ Fretted instruments

The acoustic guitar is the most common of these, but the same techniques can be used for mandolins, bouzoukis and banjos, with slight variations.

Microphone Capacitor/electret. You can record the guitar with a dynamic microphone but the low level produced will tempt you to move the microphone closer and so lose the overall tonal character of the instrument. In addition the high frequency harmonics will not be reproduced by a dynamic. A stereo pair is needed for compositions which feature the acoustic guitar as a solo instrument, but in a busy mix one microphone is perfectly adequate.

Position You will find that there are quite a few good positions for miking an acoustic, but opposite the sound hole is not one of them. Although this gives the largest signal it is also the most boomy because the air vibrating inside the body is designed to give the guitar depth of tone, not definition.

A good starting point for one microphone is about a foot away pointing at the top end of the fretboard. Another microphone pointing at the lower part of the body just to the left of the bridge added to the first gives a good stereo sound. For more variation you can orientate the first microphone towards the headstock but you will pick up more fretting noise and string squeak, especially if the strings are new.

Another favoured position for a sound which has more treble content is at head height and hanging above the guitar slightly to the bridge side of the body.

Tip A light plectrum will produce a sound which has more presence and attack when strumming.

❏ Brass and woodwind

Microphone Dynamic or capacitor/electret.

Position Unlike the live situation where separation is essential, you don't need to put the microphone actually inside the instrument.

Single instruments are usually miked up with one microphone about a foot from the instrument. The mic can be pointing towards the point where the sound is emitted, or in the case of the sax even towards the centre of the instrument if the tone is better – feel free to experiment.

For a brass section, more control on the mix is possible if there are microphones on all the instruments, but with care a good balance can be achieved with two microphones used as a cross pair from a distance of two to three feet. Moving further away the room acoustic will be increasingly audible.

Problems On some instruments the mechanical parts can become noisy, and pad noise may be heard if an overhaul is necessary. Also poor reeds and maintenance can cause tuning discrepancies.

❏ Strings

Microphone Capacitor/electret.

Position For solo violin, viola and cello, try a single microphone two to five feet from the soundboard. If orientated towards the bridge the sound will be more harsh, towards the neck a mellow tonality is usually to be found.

For double basses, the physical dimensions allow two microphones to be used – one pointing towards the body of the instrument and the other to capture the resonance of string against neck.

Problems Although they are not loud, a great variety of range and tonal variation is to be found with stringed instruments, and you often have to move the microphone for different compositions.

❏ Whistles and flutes

Microphone Dynamic for whistles, capacitor for flutes. Whistles can be surprisingly loud but also quite breathy. A capacitor microphone would emphasise all the wind noise and you would end up having to roll off the HF.

Position For whistles about six inches to a foot in front of the player. Too near the embouchure and the breath noise will be emphasised. Flutes tend to sound good with the microphone positioned about two feet above the player and half way along the instrument. Moving the microphone towards the embouchure will, like the whistle, increase the breathy quality of the sound.

Tip In common with brass instruments these need a little time to warm up to pitch so always let the musician play in the instrument a little before recording.

❏ Percussion

This now encompasses an enormous amount of instruments! Let's tackle the hand held shakers, cabasa, and tambourines first.

Microphone Capacitor /electret. These instruments produce a lot of high frequencies and are recorded to work in the upper mid and high frequency area of the mix.

Position If you're recording the instruments individually as overdubs, a single microphone about five or six feet off the ground pointing towards the playing position is a good start. It should be a foot or two away from the instrument itself.

Tip Don't go too close to the mic because when you hit the side of the instrument it can overload or result in a thumping sound. Try rolling off the bass below 100Hz to eliminate the chance of this happening and to cut out extraneous noise.

❏ Skins

You could easily be called upon to record congas, bongos, talking drums, bodhrans or even tabla in a small studio. All these drums have a unique sound and are also played in different styles. Bodhran and talking drum are played with a beater of some sort, whereas the others are played by hand and all are fairly loud.

Microphone You have a choice of dynamic or capacitor/electret. The latter will give you more definition of attack – the slap of the palm on the drum skin and also bring out any accenting on the rim of the instrument. The former tend to give a warmer bass end and will pick up less spill.

Position Some percussion instruments like bongos, congas and tabla are arranged as a pair, and if tracks are available it's preferable to use two microphones. A crossed pair one to two feet above the drums with each mic pointing at a different one will yield excellent results.

Stereo miking tabla drums – they can be miked from a short distance if spill is not a problem

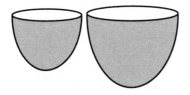

Spill is inevitable but the distance from the drum gives a more natural sound with enough separation to pan the individual drum sounds. In an ensemble situation or live you may have to resort to closer miking to prevent spill from other instruments.

For individual drums like bodhran and talking drum which are played with a beater, you can try a single microphone on the front head, behind, or both. Again a little distance from the drum may help unless you want to take advantage of the bass proximity effect of a dynamic cardioid for a punchy bass end.

Tips Some of the drums mentioned are played with the intention of changing the pitch of the drum as they are struck and adding grace notes by hitting the rim of the drum. You need to make sure that all this is being picked up, not just the main beat. The sound of the drum rim can be louder than the skin, and microphone placement must be used to alleviate this potential problem. Finally if you're used to recording drum kits, don't automatically apply the same equalisation techniques, as these percussive drums often have a different function and occupy a different place in the mix.

❏ Blues harp

Microphone Dynamic. A condenser will pick up a lot of unwanted high frequency overtones, squeaks, puffs and grunts!

Position This depends what type of sound you want. For a clean sound the player would stand about six inches from the microphone, however this is not how most blues harp players would use the mic. Usually it is hand held with the harp cupped inside the hands. Opening and closing the hands fractionally introduces changes in tone which are then easily picked up by the microphone.

Tip Run the output of the microphone into an amp (preferably valve) and mic the cabinet up. A hint of overdrive will give you the classic dirty sound of a sweaty blues band.

Miking up the blues harp through an amp

❏ The piano

You're unlikely to use one in a small studio but the grand piano is the instrument that most serious music would be played on if you get the chance to record one.

Microphone Capacitor or electret to capture the wide frequency range, coincident cardioid, spaced omnis (if you have the choice) or PZMs.
Position Two close mics would normally be used to capture the full range of the piano because it's only worth going for a room sound if the room is acoustically right.
Close miking Hanging over the top of the open lid on an upright, under the lid on a grand about six inches from the strings at the point where the hammers hit them. PZMs could be attached to the underside of the lid.
In the room On boom stands about five feet off the ground and about four feet away from the piano. PZMs could be attached to a wall, the floor or ceiling, or mounted on boards at a small distance from the piano.
Problems Check all the notes are even by playing chromatically up and down the keyboard, if not, move the microphones until it is so. Pedals and hammers can sometimes be noisy.

❏ Pickups on acoustic instruments

Can be very useful in a live situation but seldom give a true representation of the sound. The simple reason for this is that they pick up the sound from one part of the instrument – often the bridge, yet the tonal character of the instrument is a combination of different resonances best heard at a little distance.

Some equalisation can be used to recapture the natural acoustic sound, and this usually involves some modification of the upper mid to high frequencies (a little cut) and the lower mids (again a cut at around 200 – 300Hz) on stringed instruments.

❏ DI

If the pick up signal is boosted by a pre amp it can be plugged into the line input of a desk, but this is only found on the more expensive instruments. A DI box or external pre amp is usually necessary to match signal levels.

You can use a combination sound of microphone and DI, and you may well want to compare them for a given recording situation so it's always wise to try both side by side if a DI signal is available. Care must be taken to avoid phase problems if you decide to use both together, and some microphone movement may be necessary to get the signals in phase.

5 | *Some useful effects for acoustic instruments*

❑ Natural reverb

A natural reverb picked up by room mics can be really effective especially in the case of brass and percussion. Tiled halls, kitchens and bathrooms are all potential live areas, and if it is possible to record the ambient mic to a different track you can alter the sound quite radically later. Nasty frequencies of small rooms – usually in the 400 – 800Hz region can be cut using EQ, compression can be added to even dynamics and add punch, and gating used to cut the length of the reverb if it is too long.

In a small studio it is more likely that the reverb will be too short, but the decay time can be artificially lengthened using a digital reverb with a room preset and decay time of a second or so.

❑ Artificial reverb

Room reverbs between 0.6 and 1.6 seconds are useful to create a sense that someone is actually playing in a live acoustic. Equalisation is usually needed to edit the reverberation because unwanted frequencies tend to be boosted that are more noticeable on a sparse acoustic piece. Brass and percussion are well suited to this treatment.

○ PROJECT

Listen to the reverb

Record an acoustic guitar and add reverb to it on playback. Solo the reverb return channels (on most desks soloing a post fade effects return will also cut the send signal so use a pre fade send or take the left/right bus buttons out on the dry channel) and listen to the frequencies that are being affected. If certain notes are being emphasised, try to locate and cut them on the effect equalisation or the desk EQ.

It's often easier to try the desk EQ first because you can see it all at a glance then translate what you've done there to the effect EQ. This can then be stored for future use.

❏ Gated reverb

This is well suited to short, sharp percussive sounds and brass stabs where the underlying tonality of the reverb can also provide body as well as zap!

❏ Longer reverb

This is particularly suitable to wind instruments like flute and whistle which play monophonically unless overblown. A chordal instrument would soon lose clarity in the confusion of reflections that a long reverb time presents.

❏ Double tracking

A common brass treatment, the slight discrepancies in timing and tuning all aid the sound. A similar effect can be achieved using an ADT or a pitch shifter with a delay section.

❏ Pitch shifting

If you have only a small brass section and you want to fatten up the sound, try shifting the pitch up an octave with an effects unit. On the budget effects this will have a fair amount of glitching, but when mixed low enough it can fool the ear into thinking there are more players.

A stereo pitch shifter can also sound wonderful on acoustic guitar if you need a bit of fairy dust in the mix! Try these settings on a strummed acoustic:

pitch fine left	– 8 cents and down.
pitch fine right	+ 10 cents and up.
delay left	15ms
delay right	25ms

You can also get a twelve string guitar effect from a six string acoustic using a harmoniser as it samples the original and plays it back slightly out of pitch and usually with a slight delay.

Drums can also be altered in pitch on the pitch shifter, but care will need to be taken if you mix them back in with the original as the delay is audible on fast attack sounds.

❏ Tape tricks

Drums can be recorded with the tape running faster if you want a sound with a lower tone at the right speed. This is very useful for those occasions where the only drum available is a small one or has no tuning mechanism. This may require some dexterity if the piece is already fast at normal speed!

❏ Varispeed

A good varispeed is essential for recording folk instruments which are not always in perfect pitch. Temperature changes are problematic for most acoustic instruments so if you're looking at digital multitracks it's wise to check the varispeed limits are suitable.

❏ Key triggered gate

Keying one instrument from another. In this example brass stabs and guitar chords are played together, but one is locked to the other to make the sound tighter and add punch

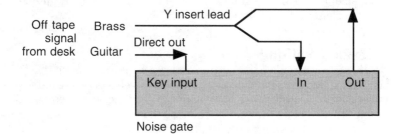

Key triggering the gate

6 Recording electric guitars

Not only are there a massive range of guitars now available, but you could be using amplifiers and cabs with microphones, direct injection boxes, pre-amplifiers or speaker simulators to get a recorded guitar sound.

❏ Which microphone?
A dynamic with a unidirectional pick up pattern is the most common choice, particularly when recording in the same room as other musicians, because it cuts spill. For a more ambient sound a capacitor with a figure of eight or omnidirectional pattern will give a more open sound, but you could always use a PZM for this job.

Incidentally, if you have a capacitor that will take the level there's no rule that says you can't use it to mic up speakers.

❏ How many do I need?
One is usually enough, but if you have the luxury to pick and choose and the amplifier is isolated from other sounds, set up as many as you like. However you very rarely end up using more than two.

❏ And the microphone position?
If you are using one microphone, position it a couple of inches away from the speaker and point it towards the centre of the cone for maximum treble, or slightly off centre to reduce it.

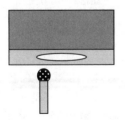

Mic placed off centre of speaker cone to reduce treble

For a more experimental set up try one in front, one behind (for open backed cabinets), one about four feet in front of the speaker cab, and one ambient about twelve feet away. On the desk you can then listen to them individually and also experiment with combinations.

You will notice that the one placed behind will have a lot more bass in the signal as the treble from a combo is directed forward. The ambient will of course pick up more of the room sound.

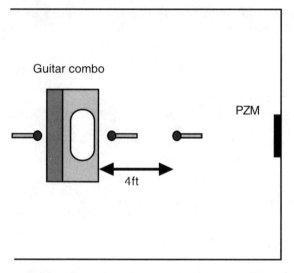

Multimiking the guitar amp

❑ **Phase cancellation**

The chances are that you will hear this when you mix the sound from two microphones together. Lift the front of amp fader to zero dB then slowly add the mic behind the speaker or the one four feet away. You should observe a change in tonal colouration that you may find useful or undesirable.

Altering the distance of the mics from the speaker will alter this tone again as the sound waves strike the microphones at different points in their cycle. An unwanted side effect can be loss of clarity.

❑ **Sound at source**

Remember to try and get the source sound as good as possible before resorting to equalisation. A well set up guitar with decent strings and good intonation is essential to avoid tonal and pitch troubles.

❑ Speaker simulators

These allow you to use the amplifier head without it being connected to the speaker(s). The stand alone units work as a combined power soak, EQ filter and DI box, converting the energy from the speaker output into a lower level balanced or unbalanced signal suitable to plug straight into the desk. This gives you the benefit of a hard run amp without the noise problems – very useful in a home studio. In addition there will be no spill in a multi microphone situation, and you also have the convenience of being able to set up the amp in the control room for overdubbing. This last ensures better communication between engineer/producer and guitarist.

Speaker simulator outputs are now fitted as standard to most good quality guitar pre-amplifiers, as manufacturers realise the need for a more natural sound. Here their role is that of equalisation to emulate the filtering effects of connecting an amp to a speaker and thus cutting the treble. As such it is of more benefit for distorted sounds than clean ones.

❑ DI (direct injection)

The direct injection (DI) box converts a high impedance signal to a low impedance one, may have some signal pad switching, an earth lift, basic filter EQ, line and speaker inputs, a choice of balanced and unbalanced outputs and accept phantom power if it's the full Monty!

More basic (and cheaper) models do exist and a DI box is an essential item for any studio where guitars are going to be recorded. You can plug them in line between the instrument and the desk to get a good clean signal, but they are problematic when used after distortion because you don't have the filtering effect of a speaker to cut the harshness from the signal. On the up side there's no spill in a multi mic situation, you get a strong signal and avoid the side effects of a mismatching impedance – low level and loss of treble.

Your amplifier could have a DI output which feeds you the signal before the filtering effect of the speaker so it's going to deliver plenty of treble. Once again this is great for clean guitar when you want the character of your own amplifier head, but tends to be fizzy when an overdrive is selected on the amp. Amplifier DI's don't cut the signal to the speaker so you could run both a microphone and a DI, but there will be a phase difference between the two signals.

On the more expensive amplifiers there will be an independent volume, but on the others you will be working at a level governed by the amp master volume, and this can sometimes be enough to overload a desk input with no pad switch.

❏ The pre-amp

You can get two types of pre-amp – one with built in effects, or just a basic model. They come in all shapes and sizes, some are rack mounted, others are built into a pedal boards, and some are so small you can even carry them in your pocket! The sheer versatility and ease of use of these units has made them popular for session guitarists, and in the small studio, where noise levels may be a problem.

You can use them with an amplifier instead of plugging direct to the desk, if you wish, because of the variable output level. Another advantage is that they can often be used as ordinary effects units on a mix by bypassing the pre-amp section.

The quality of the pre-amplification section is where they stand or fall. Digital effects for example are fine, but a digital pre-amplifier in front of them gives at best an artificial sound. If you prefer something more natural then the analogue pre-amp stages (mostly American designs) are superior and some even have valves if that's your preference.

❏ Active pickups

Because of the output level, guitars fitted with these can usually be plugged straight into the desk without any signal degradation. Apart from this benefit they shouldn't lose presence when the volume control is turned off maximum. Their one drawback is that they are noisier than non-active pickups.

❏ Bass guitars

Can benefit from all the above, but you will find that there are less products available for bass guitarists because there is a smaller market for the products – obviously there are not so many bedroom bassists!

❏ Microphones for bass guitars

Use unidirectional dynamics for close miking. You could also try some of the dedicated bass drum mics, like the AKG D112E, but a standard dynamic should do the trick. For ambient miking a capacitor is necessary, but as bass sound waves are more likely to bring a room's wave acoustics into play you may find that the room is emphasising certain notes and introducing complications.

❏ Position

Placing the mic one to two feet away from the cabinet and pointing it at the speaker will give a better result as the cabinet itself plays a big role in the sound reproduction.

❑ Speaker simulator

You can use these with bass guitars just as well as with guitars, but be careful of the amplifier power rating. The stand alone speaker simulators are built to take up to 100W, but many bass amps are rated more highly.

❑ DI

Many engineers will take a DI'd sound in preference to a microphone because it's easier to get a good sound fast, and a DI box on a non-active bass is essential to preserve the presence and level of the signal.

DI outputs on bass amp heads are common, but more often than not the level they produce is far too great for the desk when the amp is run at gig volume.

A DI box in line between the amp and desk, or a desk with a pad switch (not often found on budget consoles) may be able to handle it. Only the most expensive bass amplifiers seem to have independent output control of their DI outputs, an output which bypasses the amplifier equalisation, and will provide a mixed output when a bi-amp system is being used.

❑ Bi-amping

If you have the luxury of channels it might be nice to have control of the bass and top independently by taking outputs from both and putting them on two separate tracks. The treble channel can then be treated with a delay or modulation effect independently without the normal phase cancellation of bass frequencies on the overall sound.

❑ DI plus microphone

It is common in bigger studios to try a combination of microphone and DI signals, but phase problems can once again present a snag. As one signal reaches the desk at the speed of light (DI) and the other at the speed of sound (speaker to mic) there is a phase discrepancy which can show up as a lack of bass.

You may have noticed a similar thing if you plug a bass through a modulation pedal, an effect which uses a small time delay. This loss of bass can be rectified by moving the microphone until it is in phase with the DI signal. Larger desks have phase reversal switches which can be of value here, but few budget models are fitted with such a luxury.

❑ **Troubleshooting**

Symptom When you mic up an overdriven guitar sound and the mic is close to the speaker you seem to have more distortion in the microphone sound than you perceive in the room.

Solution This is because you don't set up the sound with your head so near the speaker! If you are otherwise happy with the microphone position, reduce the distortion amount in the amp sound. If you decide to move the microphone, try it at head height about six feet from the amp where you might normally stand to play. Unfortunately you will then lose the bass proximity effect of the microphone and will have to add bass EQ to the sound on the amp or at the desk if necessary.

Symptom The clean sound has a distinct peak frequency.

Solution If you can't guess where the problem frequency is turn the gain up on the mid sweep EQ and sweep through the frequency range until that frequency gets louder. Once found, turn the desk EQ gain to a negative position by a few dB's, or get the guitarist to do that on the amplifier's own EQ if it is so equipped and turn off the desk EQ. If all else fails use a compressor set to hard compression and a threshold set at the point where only the peak signal will cause gain reduction to occur, then adjust the ratio to suit.

Symptom There is too much noise on the signal path.

Solution Check the guitar. Are the pickups single coil and prone to pick up interference from dimmers and fluorescent lights? Is the guitarist next to an effects rack or computer screen? For all these problems you will have to find a position for the guitarist to stand where the interference is least noticeable. If lighting is not the cause check the leads and any connecting sockets like effects pedals.

On an overdriven sound with a lot of pre-amplifier gain you must expect a lot of noise, and you need to decide whether this will be heard in the mix or not. If so then it can be gated, but this need not be done until the mix stage. It will save time on the mix if your drop ins and outs are accurate when overdubbing as there will be less noise to clean up.

Symptom When track sharing between overdriven and clean guitar, the clean guitar sounds much louder even though they are both peaking at the same level.

Solution A clean sound has more cut and really should be recorded about 5dB lower than the overdriven one if you want them to appear at the same level in the mix.

Symptom The distorted guitar sound seems to hold a very steady signal level as if it was compressed.
Solution In fact the overdrive is acting as a form of compressor when it squares off those nice sine wave signals, and it is quite normal for the signal level to apparently have a fixed level when the guitarist is playing with a lot of distortion.

Symptom The guitar sound on tape has turned out to be not as good as you thought but the performance is good. Is there any way that you can keep the take but get a better sound?
Solution Yes, by running the signal out to an amplifier and miking it up again. If there are no free tracks then bring the microphone signal up on a spare desk channel for the mix. You could also run the signal to a pre amp. Choice of signal path from the desk could be via a pre fade send, an insert point send or a direct out and this gives you the option of running the original with or without the new signal.

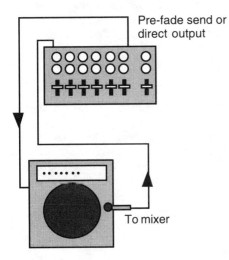

Pre-fade send or
direct output

To mixer

Sending a DI guitar to the amp for re-recording

Tip If you are worried about the guitar sound and have a spare track, take a DI of the signal at the same time as the mic or pre-amp. The clean DI will capture the performance and can more easily be used on the mix for improving a poor amplified sound. It may even sound good mixed in with the original! But remember that a good sound at source is still the best thing to aim for.

Symptom Communication is difficult with the musician playing in another room.
Solution Make a tie line between the control room and the playing area so that the guitarist can plug into the control room patchbay and connect to the amp. Use a speaker simulator or pre amplifier. Any of these solutions will work if the guitarist does not need to get feedback from the speaker in the playing area.

Symptom Can you get feedback from the studio monitors?
Solution Yes but be careful with this one as the studio monitors have to be turned up loud, so make sure they will not be damaged.

Symptom The guitarist wants to use his own effects pedals, surely the studio effects will give a better sound?
Solution They may well do for some things, noticeably reverb, but the character of the guitarist's personal sound will be altered and something original lost if you don't try the pedals first. Some songs are written around effects like tremolo (REM, the Monster album), heavy modulation (Siouxsie and the Banshees) and echo (U2), and it is important for the guitarist to hear them as they affect the performance.

Many musicians now have sophisticated set ups with good quality effects, and the producer's task is then to decide if they are appropriate for the song and get the recorded mix between them and the dry signal right.

Tip Amplifier reverb is a case where it may be better to use a studio quality effect for creating stereo and to suit the mix you have in mind.

7 Production effects for electric guitars

❑ Real double tracking

On guitar this works really well panned hard left and right to give a big stereo spread to the sound, and as such it's best saved for the choruses in songs to give extra lift. Obvious inconsistencies should be re recorded but slight innacuracies usually add to the rhythmic swing. You can also try this on bass if you want a big sound.

❑ Artificial double tracking (ADT)

If you are short of tracks but want a double tracked effect on the mix try this as a starting point:

Delay time	20 – 60ms
Feedback	single repeat
Modulation	off, or try small depth and speed.
Pan	dry and wet signals hard left and right.

❑ Tempo delay

Use this formula to determine tempo related delay speeds

60 divided by bpm = quarter note delay
divide result by 1.5 for triplet style delay

Delay can be used effectively for rhythm, or as a means of sustaining chords and notes.

❑ Non tempo related delay

Can be just as effective on the guitar as long as the repeats are not so obvious. One of the great things about tape delays was their low bandwidth which created a warm and sometimes modulated delay when the tape ran unevenly. You can recreate this on a digital unit by using a low pass filter on the effect, cutting it down to as low as 4kHz in some situations.

❏ Modulated delay

Run the output of the delay into a modulation effect. If you are using a multi-effects unit this may be an option on the internal signal path. The modulated echo will give a very big sound that is suitable only for compositions with a sparse instrumentation.

Another useful tip is to use a swell pedal or the volume control on the guitar to swell in the dry sound. This produces a wonderful wave of sustained guitar when the above effects are added and could easily be used instead of a pad keyboard.

Suggested settings to start:
If you are not using a tempo related delay time try:

delay	450ms
feedback	25%
modulation	low speed
depth	to taste

❏ Pitch change – classic fretless bass

Use a stereo pitch change with these settings varied to suit:

left pitch fine	+10 cents
right pitch fine	−10 cents
left pre delay	15ms
right pre delay	20ms

This is also good for clean guitar and mid eighties style lead guitar.

❏ Heavy rock guitar solo

For this setting the glitching of the pitch change will be audible unless it is placed back in the mix where it will still be effective.

coarse pitch	+12
minimum pre delay.	

❏ Classic Leslie guitar modulation

On an old delay unit this can sound great:

speed	fast
depth	30%
delay	15ms +
feedback	low

If you have a programmable effects unit you may be able to control the Leslie speed via MIDI controller messages for a more authentic sound.

❏ Using reverb

You don't generally need a lot of reverb on guitar unless it's for a special effect. For example the modulated delay effect outlined above could equally well be used with reverb. In this instance it might be nice to run the reverb last in the chain because of the more random nature of its reflection pattern.

❏ Pre-delay

As with drums a rhythmic pre-delay in tempo with the composition can give an interesting effect, and it will also provide stereo interest when panned to the opposite side from the guitar. Try it on short guitar stabs and pan the reverb to one side of the stereo.

❏ Gated reverb

For special effects a gated reverb is an obvious but useful ploy. The length of hold is critical – too long or short and you can throw the rhythm. Also try a backwards reverb if you don't have a multitrack that allows you to reverse the tape.

❏ Tape effects – double track with varispeed

Record the second take with the pitch slightly sharp or flat by about 5 cents and you will get the same effect as a harmoniser only without the processing delay. This is great for twelve string effects and genuine jangly pop guitar.

❏ Backwards tape

Run the tape to the point to the end of the section you want the backwards guitar to play on. Reverse the tape (remember that all your track numbers are now reversed too ie. on an eight track, track one will now appear where track eight was). Play guitar onto a free track against the backwards music, turn the tape back the right way and hey presto, backwards guitar.

It's also good to lay effects to tape backwards against guitar you have already recorded – echo and reverb in particular because their decay tails will appear to pre-empt the guitar sound.

❑ Brighter guitar

Another tried and tested method developed over twenty years ago to get a brighter, more punchy sound is to use the varispeed to drop the pitch by an octave. Play the guitar part an octave lower and then return the tape to proper pitch.

❑ Triggering the gate

Run the guitar signal into the noise gate and send the key trigger input a percussive signal. Great for dance tracks, especially on a distorted signal running into feedback.

❑ Using compressors to tape

Usually it's only needed for clean guitar where the dynamics are badly played. A threshold set to trigger gain reduction only on the peaks at a ratio between 2:1 and 5:1 should do the trick. Attack fairly fast – if you are losing the attack of the guitar itself then lengthen it on the compressor and check that your threshold is not set too low. Release should be set to fit the part being played. Start at a medium setting and adjust to suit.

❑ Sustain

Pedal compressors or 'sustainers' are often used by guitarists, but you can emulate that sound on a studio based effects unit without losing as much of the high frequency. Suggested settings:

ratio	6:1 – 10:1
attack	medium
release	long

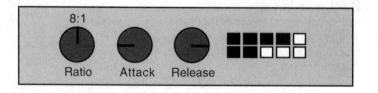

❏ Swell guitar

If you apply a lot of compression it will dip the level of the guitar attack, and the compressor can then appear to increase the level as it returns the signal to unity gain with a long release. The drawback is the amount of noise, but this can be carefully gated out using an expander gate of the type often found on rack mounting compressors.
Suggested settings:

ratio	10:1
attack	fast
release	long

❏ Slap and finger style bass

The fast attack and volume increase of slapped bass can cause problems for compressors and tape levels when alternated with finger style playing in one take. A compression that suits finger style will be vastly over compressed and lose attack for slap bass so here are some ways around the problem:

- Record on separate tracks and bounce to one track later.
- Drop in the slap bass with a different compression setting on the same track.
- Go with the level changes and split the channel on the mix for the different sections.

❏ Slap bass compression

Hard compression works better than soft knee where it is difficult to find a compromise setting between over compression and under compression.

attack	medium
ratio	4:1+
release	fast to medium

Recording drums

❏ Miking live drums
Unidirectional dynamics are most often used for kick, snare and toms in a multi mic situation to cut spill and cope with the sound level of a close miked drum. For overheads, hi-hat and room sounds capacitor, electret and PZM types will capture the high frequencies and room characteristics. As for polar patterns the hi-hat microphone will have to be unidirectional but you can be more experimental with the others.

❏ Kick drum miking
A dedicated kick drum microphone is useful because it's constructed to emphasise the low frequency thump at around 80Hz and perhaps also the attack at 2–6kHz.

❏ Snare
Capacitor microphones that can accept the high SPL are often used on the snare in professional studios.

❏ Toms
Microphones that are mounted on the actual drum rather than a stand can be helpful in a large multi - mic situation where there is not much room. However they are very close to the drum head.

❏ Don't buy – hire
You don't have to own all these microphones, hiring in may prove a cheaper alternative to buying.

❏ Three microphones or less
The famous John Bonham sound on the much sampled 'When the Levee Breaks' was accomplished with three microphones in a hall. One positioned a few feet in front of the kick drum and the other two as a stereo room pair. Even though the kick drum microphone helps to give added definition to the low frequencies, the main requirement is a good sounding room because the stereo pair will pick up the room reverb characteristics.

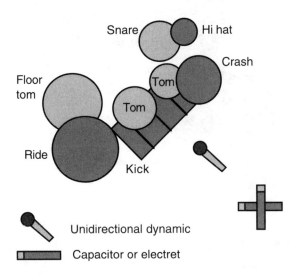

Crossed pair and kick drum mics. The kick drum mic is at the same height as the drum centre and the capacitor mics about six feet off the ground

❏ Hire a hall

If your recording equipment is mobile you can hire a hall to record drums for serious projects and mix at home. Conversely the authentic dead acoustic of seventies drums for indie dance and breakbeats requires just two or three microphones in a small room. You can damp the acoustic of the room with heavy drapes, blankets and even duvet covers!

❏ Adding effects

If you are using just two or three microphones remember that any effects you add will be on the whole drum kit. If you want more control you will have to use separate microphones routed to their own tape tracks.

❏ Multi-miking drums

With so many mics and leads it's a good idea to have a systematic approach which you can vary to suit individual requirements. For example always start with the kick drum, next the snare, then the hi hat, the toms and finally the overheads. If you're working in one studio most of the time then you may as well use the same tracks on the tape machine for drums every time.

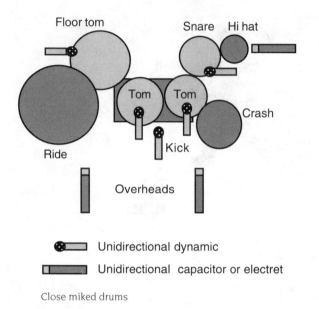

Close miked drums

❑ Avoid confusion

(a) Make sure the stage box is close to where the kit is likely to be set up for shorter leads and tidy cabling.
(b) Colour code or number the leads.
(c) Remember to make a note of the input channels you're using on the desk, and mark down the final destination of the drums on a track sheet, including the microphone for future reference.

❑ Four track

Using just a couple of microphones for four track is easier, but if you want to try more you will probably need a desk to submix the drums and add effects live. It's a good idea to try and record the entire rhythm section to stereo tracks if recording a band, but for overdubbing you may be limited to one track.

❑ Effects tip

If the drums are recorded in mono, stereo effects like reverb will spread the sound if added on the mix rather than to tape.

❏ Eight track

For eight track recording you face a compromise. It's initially better to record the kick drum and snare drum onto separate tracks if possible as they are often the most important sounds to get right in pop and rock recording. Try this:

1	Kick
2	Snare
3	Stereo toms and overheads (left)
4	Stereo toms and overheads (right)

When other instruments have been recorded like bass guitar and guitar on tracks five and six respectively, you can bounce the drums to stereo on tracks seven and eight. The other instruments will provide a reference to their mix. Also any compression, gating and reverb effects can then be added in a more controlled situation during the sub mix.

❏ Submixing

In a situation where a large set of toms has to be mixed, remember that relative tom levels are critical – in effect you're mixing them straight away and mistakes are hard to rectify later.

Although it may sound obvious, selecting one odd/even tape assign button for the toms and one for the overheads does make life simpler if you are using subgrouping to send the signal to tape. You can then use the pan controls for stereo tom positioning.

❏ Sixteen track

I would probably designate tape tracks like this for a straightforward set up:

1	kick drum
2	snare
3	stereo toms (left)
4	stereo toms (right)
5	overhead (left)
6	overhead (right)
7	hi hat

The appearance of the hi hat on track seven is because the toms are submixed. If you've got enough tracks for the drums then by all means assign the toms to individual tracks using direct outputs on the tape and place the hi hat where you like! A more complex routing example could be:

1	kick
2	snare top
3	snare bottom
4	hi hat
5	tom 1
6	tom 2
7	floor tom
8	overhead (left)
9	overhead (right)

In this example a microphone has been added to the underside of the snare for a bigger sound choice on the mix, but two microphones could easily have been used in the first example and subgrouped to one tape track with attention to levels.

❏ Kick drums – microphone positions and EQ

The kick drum is usually double headed with a hole cut in the front head. This hole is often big enough for a microphone on a low boom stand to have access inside the drum itself. If the hole is small you can still put a microphone to it but you will end up with a sound with more sustain, not necessarily a bad thing. Some drummers take the whole front head off if there is no hole, but make sure that they take the lugs that hold the head onto the main drum off too otherwise they'll rattle! You can successfully mic up a double headed kick drum but must accept more spill from the rest of the kit.

❏ Kick drums – tuning and damping tips

New heads help a lot but it's very expensive to rehead a kit, especially the kick drum so it's unlikely that the drummer will have more than a spare snare head.

To get a lot of punch and a good clicky attack detune the skin and use a wooden or hard felt beater. Nevertheless inexperienced drummers may find it hard to play without a tight springy tuning so you may have to reach a compromise.

Another way of getting top out of a kick drum is to use a plastic pad (available from drum shops) stuck to the head where the beater makes contact with the skin.

Kick drums are invariably damped with pillows, foam, and the drummer's towel, otherwise they sound like the Salvation Army. Your job is to make sure that it is not under or over-damped, so if you can hear a longish boomy note then you know that more damping is needed!

❑ Mic positioning

Placing the mic inside the drum about 10cm from the point where the beater makes contact with the head will give you lots of upper mid click and also a good bass response. This position also gives the greatest amount of separation, reducing the spill from the other parts of the kit. It is also the most artificial when equalised, gives the shortest note and sounds most like a drum machine if that's what's required.

This short bass note can be altered in the mix by bringing up the level of the overheads or artificially lengthened using a reverb, but, for a natural long note and more real drum sound, position the microphone in line with the front of the drum. Another microphone positioned a few feet in front of the drum and compressed in the mix is also used occasionally in bigger studios.

❑ Equalisation

The kick drum operates in the 20Hz – 10kHz range, with the majority of the energy located in the 20 – 200Hz region. As the microphone is in such an unnatural place some EQ is necessary. Try boosting by a few dB at 2 – 6kHz for more attack, and cutting around 250Hz if the drum sound is too hard.

❑ Snare drum

Whether metal, wooden or a combination of both, the snare can often prove to be difficult. Sometimes two microphones are needed on the deep military snares favoured by heavy rock drummers in order to capture the sound of the snare itself as well as the top skin.

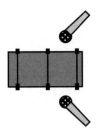

Two mics capture sound from snare as well as from top skin

❏ Snare drum – tuning and damping tips

Invariably the snare will rattle sympathetically when one of the toms is hit unless the drummer is really ace at tuning. If this is unavoidable then you always have the option of using a noise gate on mixdown to eliminate the rattle.

Metal snares in particular are likely to produce an unmusical clang if they're not damped, but avoid over damping unless you want the snare to sound more like a suitcase of socks!

The snare drum itself has an internal damper which may be put in contact with the top head. If this sounds bad or is insufficient then try cutting the centre out of an old or broken snare head until about an inch is left around the edge and place this on the head. Alternately you can buy the commercially produced kind.

Yet another method is to place your finger lightly on the drum skin then hit the drum and keep repeating until you find the annoying overtone. Place some gaffa tape or stick a bit of rag to the spot where your finger was (this principle can equally well be applied to toms by the way).

❏ Getting the sound

On the subject of tuning remember you don't have to use a sampler to get the sound. For example ballads often have a deeper snare, rock requires a tightish tuning with a lot of attack, ska has a clanging metal snare, dance snares are struck lightly with a lot of snare in the sound and jazz often uses a tightly tuned drum.

❏ Positioning the snare mic

A couple of inches away from the head is best. Very close miking will give you a lifeless sound. Also angle the microphone so that it's pointing towards the centre of the snare, after all that's where the drum tone will have been tuned to sound best. An alternative position I've found useful is almost horizontally near the edge of the snare but still pointing towards the centre.

> Tip Don't point the microphone at a place where the snare is damped, and don't put the mic where the drummer is likely to hit it with a stick (especially if you're using a capacitor – ouch!).

Remember that a lot of hi-hat is likely to bleed down the snare mic so try and angle the microphone away from the it.

Likewise watch what you do with the treble because if it's boosted it will also bring up the level of the hi-hats and increase the chance of phasing problems. Likewise, boosting bass can bring up the kick drum spill, so care must be taken here too.

The snare drum operates in the frequency range 200Hz – 10kHz with most of its energy in the lower part of that area. If more upper mid is required, experiment with cutting the bass a little so that the upper mid is apparently louder, rather than going for the boost straight away.

I've also noticed that a slight cut at 1kHz will bring out the actual sound of the snare in the higher frequencies if you've only used a top mic on the drum.

❏ Toms

There are two main sorts – double headed or single headed (concert toms). Double headed toms seem to be favoured by most session drummers because of the superior sound quality and projection, but they have to be miked from above, whereas single headed toms can be miked from underneath and inside the tom – thus increasing the separation. However you may also come across Roto Toms which have no shell and can therefore be miked from above or beneath.

❏ Toms – tuning and damping tips

Some drummers tune their toms in musical intervals of a fourth according to size. Try singing 'On Ilkley Moor Bart 'at' (if your musical theory is dodgy the last two notes are a fourth apart).

Most toms ring a little, especially if they're mounted on the kick drum, and an alternative support would help alleviate the problem. However personally I have no problem with some ring on toms. If you do have to damp them, at least make sure that all the note lengths are similar.

❏ Mic positioning for toms

If you're miking from above, favour the centre and not the edge of the tom. If the drummer has a lot of toms and microphones are limited then you're forced to mic from above and share one microphone between two toms wherever possible by placing it above the edge of them both. This may require a little tom adjustment on the part of the drummer and you must then be very careful that one tom is not louder than the other, even with the microphone in the central position. Remember the more microphones the greater the chance of phase cancellation via spill – but try explaining that to a drummer!

❑ EQ'ing toms

Floor toms can be tuned very low indeed, so there's quite a range of frequencies which can be affected by EQ. For a warm, tom sound try cutting the lower mid frequencies a little at around 200 – 400Hz. For clarity and punch adding 2 – 6kHz will usually do the trick. With new skins and well tuned toms you may find that you don't need to use equalisation at all!

❑ Hi-hats

To obtain a good sound it is essential that these are good quality. Cheap ones can sound like dustbin lids! Thirteen inch hats (like Paiste New Beats) record really well and don't spill down the other microphones as much because they're not so loud. All too often drummers turn up with the set they use live which are always incredibly loud and, being larger, of a deeper pitch so you have to use more equalisation.

❑ Mic positioning for hi-hats

Try just above or below where the hi hats meet. Don't put the microphone too far in unless you want to hear the click of the stick making contact with the top cymbal. Often you can hear a harmonic overtone from the hi-hat, and the microphone should be repositioned until this disappears. If it persists check the way the drummer plays the hat – nine times out of ten he will be holding them too tightly together which tends to bring out this overtone. Adjust the hats until they're very slightly open.

❑ EQ'ing hi-hats

If you've got the right microphone in the right place then all that's necessary is a bass roll off.

❑ Overheads

Cymbals can range from the tiny splash to the aggressively loud China-type. Again a good brand usually gives a good result.

❑ Tuning tips for overheads

Tune to the drummer's taste but try and suit the decay time of crash cymbals to the tempo of the track. Tthat is, a short decay time for a fast tempo and a long for a slow. Ride cymbals with rivet cymbals are to be avoided, unless you're going for a retro sound, as they give a constant sizzle in the HF range which is really quite annoying (goodbye to clarity). Also watch out for the really loud bells on heavy ride cymbals.

❏ Mic positioning for overheads

Mics should be equidistant from the sound source to avoid phase problems, they could be right over the kit or slightly to the front or back and should favour the cymbals if directional. If the drummer has a lot of cymbals then care must be taken with their overall sound balance. Get the drummer to hit them one after the other while you listen over the monitors. If the ride cymbal is not cutting through you may need another microphone. I usually find that the ride bleeds down the floor tom microphone enough to compensate. If you do use the PZM type suspended from stands over the kit, they will have a natural bass roll off because of their design. For a more robust sound stick them to the ceiling, the wall behind the kit or even the floor.

❏ EQ'ing overheads

The role of the overheads is more than just picking up the cymbals. It captures the whole of the kit sound from a small distance away and therefore sounds more natural than the close miked version. With a good balance between all the microphones you should be able to achieve a good drum sound and anything you do to equalise the overheads will consequently affect the rest. A little bass roll off may be necessary to preserve clarity in the bass end of the kit mix.

❏ Spill

The main sources of spill are likely to be the cymbals if they are positioned too close to the toms, the snare over all the mikes and the hi-hats down the snare mic. The main problem with this spill is that it can upset the overall balance of the kit and introduce phase cancellation, especially when you start introducing equalisation. However spill is very rarely a problem if the drummer is good and the kit is well tuned.

9 Drum production techniques and effects

❏ Live drum reverb treatments

Stereo microphones in a live room are often heavily compressed, averaging out the level of the drums, emphasising the room reverb characteristics and adding punch to the sound. This compression can be applied to tape or on the mix.

The resultant drum sound can then be run through a noise gate to determine the length of the reverb using the gate hold and decay time controls. This gives you the classic real gated drum sound so favoured in the eighties on tracks like 'In the Air Tonight' by Phil Collins.

Live room mics

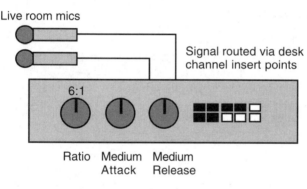

Signal routed via desk channel insert points

6:1

Ratio   Medium   Medium
        Attack   Release

Compressing the live room mics will add punch and a medium attack time will prevent the actual drum sound losing it's aggressive edge.

❏ Artificial reverb

Gate reverb is often used on drums and can emulate the above effect with a decay that has a sharp cut off point. Make the gate reverb a musical note length in tempo with the song to avoid sounding stilted and throwing the rhythm out.

○ *PROJECT*

Combined gate and hall reverb

A multi effects unit with an audio trigger and combined reverb patch is the easiest way to do this, but it can be also done with two separate reverbs running a noise gate between the aux send and the long reverb input. Set the audio threshold (or noise gate threshold) so that it is only exceeded by the snare fills on a drum track. Gate reverb will be audible on the drums all the time but a longer hall reverb (try 1.6s decay) will trigger only on the fills, adding to the energy and excitement.

❑ Room, short hall and plate

These are the reverbs most commonly used for drums in an up-tempo song. The decay time is best between 0.6 and 1.6s If the snare is not isolated by a noise gate all the other drums will get a little reverb when you turn up the effects send on the snare because of spill (which may be useful depending on the amount of hi-hat spill). If you gate the snare be prepared to add toms and a small amount of bass drum to the effects send mix.

❑ Keep it clean

If you use more reverb on the bass drum you will muddy the low frequency end of the mix. Using a high pass filter at around 80Hz will improve clarity.

A dull snare can be improved using a plate reverb with full bandwidth to imply the treble missing from the actual drum.

○ *PROJECTS*

Two reverb rhythm

Set up a short and longer reverb on two different effects units. Using a straight eights backbeat with the snare on beats two and four add the shorter reverb on beat two snare and the longer one on beat four. This gives a push pull momentum to the track and is a common producer's trick found on many recordings.

Tip If you don't have automation this will be impossible to do on the mix so record the reverb to a spare tape track.

Pre delay reverb

Find the bpm value of a song (see table below) and convert it to a millisecond delay time. This can then be used on the drums, particularly the snare, to give a lilting effect to the rhythm. Try it on a straight beat at 120bpm with a 125ms pre delay.

T*ip* Panning the dry sound to one side and the wet to another gives the impression that the sound is flying across the stereo field on each trigger!

Tempo/BPM table

Tempo (in BPM)	Crotchet (1/4)	Quaver (1/8)	Semi quaver (1/16)	1/2 4/4 bar	1 4/4 bar	2 4/4 bar
130	462	231	115	923	1846	3692
120	500	250	125	1000	2000	4000
110	546	273	136	1092	2184	4368
100	600	300	150	1200	2400	4800
90	667	333	167	1333	2667	5333

Delays in milliseconds

○ PROJECT

Hi-hat echo

Popularised by Stuart Copeland of the Police using real hi-hats, echo is also great on drum machine hats.

Feed an eighth note hi-hat pattern at 120 bpm to a stereo delay with the left delay at 333ms and the right at 500ms. Alter the feedback to suit and listen to that hi-hat swing!

❏ Hi-hat phase and flange

For rave and techno hats try:

delay	0.5 – 5ms
feedback	variable, moving from anti phase to phase is a nice touch.
speed	slow
depth	90%

❏ Cause a riot!

Take this sound and feed it to a dynamic filter EQ with the modulation rate in time with the track for absolute mayhem!

10 Vocals – recording and production techniques

Always remember that in a song the vocal is the most important part! Musicians will undoubtedly focus on the backing, but for the majority of the listening public the melody line and the vocal style are the first things that interest them. Record companies and producers are naturally aware of this and make a point of listening hard to the vocals so it's doubly important to get them right!

Vocal performance can vary in dynamic range from a scream to a whisper, and many singers have no concept of microphone technique, so it's up to the engineer and producer to capture the performance on tape.

❏ Which microphone?

Vocals can sound better with a good capacitor or electret microphone, but these are invariably expensive and many require a phantom power supply for their internal pre amplifiers. The AKG C1000 is an example of a reasonably priced electret which can be phantom or battery powered and has some of the benefits of a good capacitor. However many artists like David Bowie and U2's Bono have recorded vocals using a good quality dynamic microphone such as the Shure SM58, which requires no external power supply and is considerably cheaper.

It's true that not all of us have the luxury of being able to afford the microphone of our choice, but remember that you can always hire one for occasions that warrant the expense. If you go this far, check the specifications and watch out for certain pencil style capacitor microphones which may look good on paper but are extremely sensitive and easily overloaded by a vocalist.

❏ Tonal characteristics

Whatever you choose, remember that all microphones add their own tonal characteristics to the sound. If all your work is with the same singer it's worth testing a few to find the one that suits them best. For example, if a vocalist is a little sibilant on 'S' sounds, then there's little point in using a capacitor microphone which will faithfully reproduce the higher frequencies where the sibilance is most noticeable!

❏ Where do you stand?

Vocalists should stand up, facing the microphone at a distance of about ten inches. In a sitting position, a singer's diaphragm is constricted, which can cause problems with vocal projection.

The polar pattern of the microphone is usually unidirectional for singing because the vocal sound loses clarity when unwanted sound reflections are also picked up. These reflections, particularly from walls can add unwanted tonal colouration to the sound. Hard surfaces close to the microphone are out too because the sound waves bounce back that much quicker, introducing a phase like effect.

With this in mind it's often a good idea to have an acoustically deadened area for singing. A DIY approach could be to hang a sleeping bag on the wall behind the singer. In a professional studio a heavy curtain or acoustically treated sound booth is often used, but don't let this discourage you from experimenting with a more open vocal sound for special effects.

○ PROJECT

Vocal tricks

Record the voice in a live area (a hallway, kitchen, bathroom or empty room for example) standing about a foot away from the microphone. On playback notice how the room reverberation affects the sound. If you have a sweep mid equalisation you might also try to find out where this tonal colouration is most strong.

To do this, turn up the EQ gain and sweep through the mid band until the room's effect is most audible. Now try cutting the EQ gain and notice how your equalisation work has also been affecting the vocal quality. Try recording in a more acoustically dead area. How does this affect the sound?

If a more intimate sound is required, the vocalist can sing from two to three inches away from the mic, but for loud vocals this is unsuitable as it could overload the microphone. However, being closer will lead to an increase in bass if you are using a unidirectional pickup pattern (polarity) mic. This is known as the bass proximity effect and could be beneficial, depending on the tonal qualities of the voice and how the sound sits with the instrumental backing. It will also give an increased chance of 'popping' the microphone.

○ *PROJECT*

Getting closer

Starting at a distance of about a foot, talk or sing into the microphone and record while gradually moving closer to the mic. On playback there will be an obvious increase in level but also notice the increase in bass.

❑ Problems with 'popping'

This is actually caused by the push of air from the mouth on words with the letters B, P and to a lesser extent H, T and W. To protect the microphone from these unreasonably high increases in sound pressure level (SPL for short) you can use a commercial pop shield (expensive) or build your own Blue Peter style (cheap) to break up the rush of air. A coat hanger and pair of tights is the usual method . Bend the coat hanger to shape with a loop about five inches in diameter over which you stretch the toe of the tights, cut and knot the excess. If you don't normally wear tights or are too embarrassed to acquire them then kitchen utensils can also come in handy. A sieve or strainer will do the trick, but will be less aesthetically pleasing, especially if there's some old cabbage left in it!

○ *PROJECT*

Popping practice

A good singer can control popping with a slight pursing of the lips on words beginning with B or P. You can practice this over the microphone with some headphones on or without a microphone by putting your hand in front of your face and feeling the air pressure on your palm (warning – you may require mouthwash for the latter method!)

❑ Too much bass?

So you want the intimate vocal sound but with the singer so close to the microphone there's too much bass in the signal. First try moving off mic a little. If this gets rid of the bass problem but loses the intimacy move back to the microphone and see if it has a bass roll off switch. This filter gradually lessens the amount of signal from a fixed bass frequency down. 80Hz is a good choice as it gets rid of rumble and decreases the chance of popping too. If the microphone has no bass filter then there's a chance that your desk has one. If not then use the low frequency (LF) control and turn it down by 3–5 dB.

❏ Signal level to tape

Always look for the peak signal by asking the vocalist to sing what they consider to be the loudest bit of the song. You can then set your desk input gain and multitrack tape level to suit. A compressor may be useful if the dynamic gain changes radically, but a good singer should back off the microphone for the loud bits.

○ PROJECT

One for the singer

This is a project for the singer to try. Set the microphone up in a position where you can see the tape machine and operate the desk. Sing or talk into the microphone (remembering to turn the studio monitors down first and use headphones if you need to hear the signal to avoid feedback) and watch the level to tape. Sing closer to the microphone then move back a bit and sing louder. Try and make the meter reading similar for both the loud and quiet sections. Congratulations, you are now practising good microphone technique!

❏ Studio psychology

What makes a good vocal take? In my experience a lot depends on how the singer is feeling at the time because after all, music is a medium which communicates via emotion, and the singer is the one putting this across to the listener. Studio mood is therefore important. Some singers don't like to be seen when they're singing because they find it intimidating, so singing in the control room is difficult for them, as is the fish bowl effect of singing in a playing area where they can be seen through the studio window.

Others find it difficult to use large expensive condenser mics when they've been used to touring with a hand held microphone for ages. In such a case you can try just that, as long as there is not too much handling noise. In all cases it pays to try and create the right atmosphere for the artist if a good take is the result.

❏ The headphone mix

Another thing that really determines how well a vocalist sings is the foldback mix, and believe it or not a good headphone mix is a rare luxury even in professional studios! Having a stereo mix helps because then the vocal can be placed in the centre of the stereo and will not be fighting against any conflicting sounds which should be panned.

For monitoring purposes it's quite usual to have some basic vocal reverb in the headphones, but if the singer wants a particular effect like echo, always store the patch – it will alter the way they sing in terms of note length and dynamic. This patch or an edited version of it will almost definitely be needed for the mix because effects are very rarely committed to tape on the same track as the vocal.

❑ Monitor on headphones if necessary

To achieve a good headphone mix put the headphones on yourself and turn the main studio speakers off. You can instantly hear if there's a problem with the mix or if there's a fault in the headphone foldback system. Some producers wear headphones during the vocal take too so that they can understand exactly what it is that the singer is hearing when they ask for any level changes. Soloing the foldback sends over the main monitor speakers is a less critical and empathetic method of doing the same.

Some desks allow you to route the left/right mix to the headphones which can save a lot of effort, but if the singer wants his own level high it will sound out of context and difficult to evaluate in the control room.

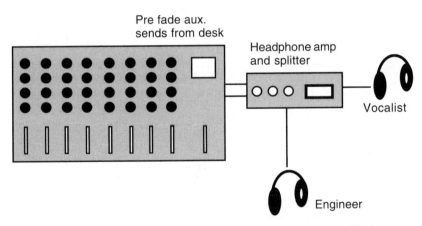

It is important for the engineer to be able to hear what the foldback mix is like for the performer

❑ Problems with headphones

Sometimes singers have problems with pitching when they are wearing enclosed headphones and can start singing a little sharp. My advice is always to pull one side of the cans slightly behind the ear to enable the vocalist to hear the sound of his own voice naturally as well as from the headphone mix. This makes it easier to correct the pitching.

❑ Non enclosed headphones

You may wonder if the non enclosed style of headphones would be a better choice, but these have several drawbacks. First you get more spill down the microphone; second they're not loud enough for some singers; and third they are more prone to feedback. Enclosed cans are also guilty of this when singers in the process of taking them off accidentally hold them next to the microphone – and we all know what happens when you point a microphone at a speaker that's carrying the microphone signal!

A phase problem can also occur if the cans are too loud and the vocal is particularly loud in the mix, as there is a slight delay between the time the vocal sound waves hit the microphone and the time the version spilling from the headphones does. To be honest this is rare but one vocalist I recorded had a nasty habit of holding one of the headphones slightly away from his head with predictably phased results which I thought initially were room reflections until I found out what he was doing!

❑ Recording without headphones

Many famous vocalists like Annie Lennox, Bono and Sade don't use headphones at all, preferring to sing acoustically to a backing played through the control room monitors, but doesn't this cause immense problems with spill? Well that really depends on how loud the monitoring is and you'll be surprised at what you can get away with, because spill is only a problem when the vocal is isolated. However there is the old reverse phase trick to fall back on.

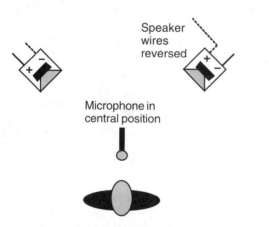

Using out of phase monitors to minimalise spill

○ PROJECT

Phase cancellation

Reverse the speaker connections on one of the speakers. Place microphone on stand equidistant from speakers. Play backing track in mono. Wearing headphones to monitor what the microphone is picking up, adjust the position of the microphone for maximum phase cancellation of the backing track. Record vocal.

❑ Composite vocals (comping)

Record up to three takes all the way through if you have enough tracks, even if the singer makes a mistake or two. The first take will have the most spontaneity, the second most control, and by the third the singer may be getting bored, but there could still be some good moments. Make a note of the best lines on each and see if there are enough to make up a good composite take. If so bounce the vocal 'comp' to a clear track.

If you can't afford the tracks for this, let the singer listen and discuss the first take. Any glaring errors can usually be rectified on a second take and bad lines repaired by dropping in. Never try and record a song line by line because the singing will soon lose any feel as the vocalist gets more and more uptight every time you stop and point out a mistake!

❑ Double track the vocals

It's not unusual to double track the chorus when the main vocal sounds a little thin. This will give it a thicker sound and the occasional inaccuracy can work in your favour, especially if you equalise or use a different effect on the double tracked voice. You may also notice a slight chorusing or phase effect occurring between the two vocals as a result of slight pitching inaccuracies – this is quite usual and one of the things that really fattens the sound up. It also makes this real double tracking more effective than the artificial method using a delay for ADT.

To save time if you intend to go for the double tracking approach make sure that each chorus is sung in a similar way, give or take the odd line or two. This makes it easier to track up, otherwise all the variations on each chorus have to be painstakingly followed!

Occasions where a double tracked vocal doesn't work are when the lead vocal is sung with plenty of character and the singer has a good, strong voice. Double tracking then tends to blur the lead vocal detail and the personality of the performance is lost.

○ *PROJECT*

Double tracking tips

Record a section of lead vocal, then double track it. Balance it so that it's at a slightly lower level than the main vocal and listen to the effect. Run the section again and try different equalisations and effects on the backing vocal, being as extreme as you like. Also try listening to the second voice at different levels.

❏ Multi track the vocals

With a small multitrack the idea of tracking up vocals may be hard to entertain, but it can help to give you a bigger production sound. Provided you have a two track machine or sampler it's not that hard .

1   Record a mix of the backing for the section you intend to multitrack (eg. the chorus) in mono or stereo to your two track machine. Make sure that you have a few bars of music running up to the section as a cue.
2   Wind the multitrack tape on until you have some free space.
3   Bounce the two track backing to mono or stereo on the multitrack machine.
4   Record your multitracked vocal harmonies on the spare tracks alongside the backing.
5   Mix the multitracked vocals to your two track machine or sampler.

Tips: Mix to a two track machine as a back up even when using a sampler. Remember that this is now your backing vocal mix so you need to be careful with the levels. If you don't have a two track machine which synchronises to multitrack or a sampler, run off some of the instrumental backing on the few bars leading up to the multitracked singing, then mute it before the singing starts. This will help serve as a timing reference when you are spinning in the vocal.

6   Rewind the multitrack to your original song and put in a memory point a few bars before the section you're bouncing to.
7   Play the multitrack and the two track machines together and spin in the multitracked voices to the track or tracks of your choice.

As the machines won't be running at the same speed you need to run both and by trial and error line them up to start at a point where they will be in sync for the vocal sections. This is not as difficult as it sounds!

❏ Start the multitrack first

On a reel to reel two track you can use a chinagraph to mark a starting point at, for example, one bar before the singing and hit play on the two track fractionally before the same bar comes up on the multitrack. You can then listen to the timing of the two and run them again adjusting your two track start position until it is right. If the two track starts going slightly ahead of the beat an old engineer's trick is to place a finger lightly on the left spool to slow down the speed. On a cassette machine you really have to watch the counter and try different points but it really isn't that hard once you get the hang of it.

The sampler owner has the easiest job, as the multitrack vocal can be triggered from a keyboard or sequencer synchronised to tape – and in fact need never actually be recorded to the multitrack, but run live on the mix!

❏ Recording speech

You could easily find yourself recording speech for an advertising jingle, play, book or tuition cassette say for a foreign language. This voice over work has some basic requirements:

The acoustic should be dry unless you're actually trying to use a natural reverberation. However this is usually added using artificial processing.

A good capacitor microphone with a good bass response as well as a quality high frequency reproduction will give you that quality BBC sound. Fattening up the bass end and improving the presence with EQ could be attempted with a cheaper mic but never quite sounds the same.

You will also need editing equipment. A two track reel to reel with an edit switch to lift the tape to the head would be the minimum requirement. Most voice over studios are investing in digital editing equipment these days which can cut and paste, carry out non destructive edits and timestretch the program material to suit the requirements of the client. Certainly it makes the job of editing out bad takes, clicks, coughs and unwanted noises a lot simpler.

It also reduces the need for compression by allowing normalisation of the signal, reducing the peaks and bringing everything up to an even, high level. Without such a tool, some form of compression will undoubtedly be used on record. For more subtle jobs a low threshold and a 1:5 compression ratio should be ample. For more extreme examples like adverts and jingles you may want to monitor your mix through a compressor at a high ratio of say 15:1 on small speakers, as this is what will happen to it on the radio and television broadcast. In this way you'll be able to tell if it sounds good or not.

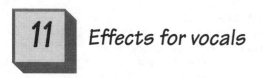

11 Effects for vocals

❏ Compressing the signal

To keep the dynamic level in check, a small amount of compression on the signal before it goes to tape can be useful. Soft knee or over easy compression is more suitable for vocals because it slightly compresses the signal all the time and is more subtle in the loud sections.

Suggested settings:

threshold	exceeded only in loud section
ratio	from 2 to 5:1
attack	fast
release	medium

❏ Aggressive compression

Can be used for that Kate Bush or Phil Collins style vocal and you should experiment with over easy and hard compression. This will affect not only the attack of the sound which should be sharp, but will also bring out the breathy quality of the vocalist.

Suggested settings:

threshold	exceeded most of the time
ratio	from 4 to 10:1 depending on how extreme you want the effect
attack	fast
release	medium to fast

The attack time can be slowed if obvious dipping in level of the sung words occurs. If you find that the effect is still too extreme, try making the threshold higher or lowering the compression ratio. Remember that if you apply this in record you cannot change it at a later date. So sometimes it is better to make this decision at the mix stage, although there is a chance that it will bring up the level of tape hiss on an analogue recording.

❏ One is not enough!

Finally there are times where a singer has such a great range in dynamic level that one compressor on its own just can't cope! In dealing with the louder sections the signal sounds over compressed but is just right for the rest of the singing.

The problem is solved by chaining two compressors together, the output of one going to the input of another. As many compressors now come in a one-U case as a stereo pair, you could use one mono side to feed the other. The second compressor should be set with a fast attack and a threshold that is exceeded only on the loud notes. This will therefore catch the problem high signals.

❏ De-essing

You hardly ever need to do this if you've used the right microphone and avoided overcompression.

In the absence of a dedicated de-esser, you can use an equaliser on the side chain of a compressor to emphasise the sibilant frequencies (boost 2 – 8kHz), and the compressed version of the signal will then have less sibilance. If you don't have an external EQ, it can be done with a spare desk channel.

❏ Reverb on vocals

To create the effect of a lot of reverb on a voice yet retain its apparent up front place in the mix, use a pre-delay on the vocal reverb. Many vocal reverb presets have a 45ms or more pre-delay already built in so your brain can distinguish the reverberation as separate from the dry sound, not mixed in with it. This improves clarity too.

❏ Gated reverb

A second microphone for vocals in a fairly live area can be positioned to pick up the room reverb (see pic overleaf), then compressed heavily and gated to achieve an interesting and aggressive vocal sound. This can then be mixed alongside the dry vocal.

❏ Triggered reverb

Using two microphones in a live room as described above, the second mic could be gated in such a way that the threshold of the gate is not exceeded until the loud bits of singing. This will give a more intimate vocal for the quiet sections but a more energetic sound with natural reverb for the loud bits.

This can be emulated on a reverb unit with an audio threshold

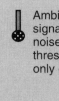

Ambient microphone signal processed by noise gate with threshold opening only on loud sections

Close mic

trigger by setting the threshold above the quiet sections. On some multi-effects units, gate reverb can run all the time and a longer reverb of say two seconds triggered when the threshold is exceeded.

❏ Catching vocal delays

There are a few methods of doing this but the method I prefer, when the vocal is not being sent to the echo in isolation, is to turn up the echo send on the vocal channel for the word or phrase you want to repeat.

If the vocal is the only sound being delayed, the master auxiliary button can be switched in and out quickly to send the signal to the delay. This is certainly easier to do in the heat of the moment while mixing! If you have MIDI control of the desk this movement can be recorded.

❏ Riding vocal sustain with delay

Where a note is held by the vocalist, a common trick is to push up the effect return fader slowly to increase the dynamic energy. A long delay setting, preferably in time with the track with about 50% feedback, will yield the best results. If you have a stereo or multitap delay it will sound even better.

❏ Expansive vocal

A combination of delay and reverb is used for this. The delay, which should be above 120ms is fed to a long reverb of 2.4s or more.

❏ Slapback delay

You may laugh but the old rock and roll cliche of 120ms + delay with one repeat is excellent for rock vocals too. I think it must be the live gig style quality of the sound that makes it work.

❏ Modulated delay

I couldn't let this pass, after all John Lennon put his vocal through a Leslie cabinet for the Beatles' 'Revolution' album. Prince often uses modulation in combination with delay and reverb.

❏ Fashion

It was once fashionable to use a heavy pitch shift patch for vocals (remember Duran Duran?). This setting uses an extreme pre-delay which can be altered to suit:

left pitch fine	+10 cents
right pitch fine	−10 cents
left delay	50ms +
right delay	70ms +

Pitch drops of an octave or more are still much used in the movies whenever a monster has to speak!

❏ Dry vocals

It is now fashionable to have an almost dry vocal sound, but next year, who knows?

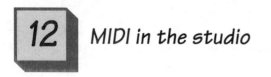

12 MIDI in the studio

❏ The advantages of tape synchronisation

1 For the small multitrack, more free tape tracks are a luxury that can lead to a better and bigger production sound. With the sequencer taking care of the bulk of the recording, there are tracks available for harmony vocals and special effects as well as conventional instruments.

2 All the sequenced parts will run live on the mix and record first generation to the master tape – a big increase in overall sound quality.

3 Any of the automation benefits a sequencer might bring can help your mix sound and increase engineer objectivity. These include program, controller and system exclusive management of sound modules, samplers, drum machines, desk mute patches, tape machines and MIDI effects processors.

❏ Different time codes

FSK, SMPTE and its MIDI equivalent – MTC – are all used in the studio, with a variety of drum machines and sequencers, although it seems that MTC is destined to become the standard for MIDI users.

❏ FSK

Most FSK units now have MIDI song position pointers which allow two devices to find a common starting place in a song. MIDI clock generated by the sequencer is converted into a stream of pulses by the FSK unit and recorded onto one track of the tape machine. On playback the synchroniser reads the code on tape, converts it back to MIDI clock information complete with SPP, and the sequencer (now in external clock mode) locks in to the appropriate sixteenth note. This usually takes a second or two to happen – longer if the sequencer has to chase the code position.

❏ Advantages of SPP

You don't have to go from the top every time as you used to do with the old FSK generators, it's an inexpensive method of tape synchronisation, and it requires little setting up. For example if you have any tempo changes, the stream of pulses sent to tape changes speed too, so on playback the sequencer MIDI clock speed will alter. This is considerably easier than programming tempo changes into a stand alone SMPTE unit. However the drawback is that once FSK code is committed to tape you cannot alter the clock rate later as you can with SMPTE.

❏ SMPTE and MTC

The actual SMPTE code that is recorded to tape contains information relating to hours, minutes, seconds, frames and sub frames. There are four frame rates available because of the differing standards between North America, Japan and Europe, and a block of code is recorded for each frame which enables the frame itself to be fractionalised for greater accuracy. These frame rates are:

```
24 fps      film
25fps       EBU
30fps       NTSC – American and Japanese b/w
30drop (29.97fps) NTSC colour
```

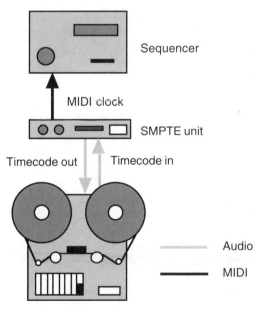

Using an external SMPTE unit for tape synchronisation

❏ Advantages of SMPTE

The system is not tempo related so the only thing you need to define before recording code is your frame rate, after which you can read the code off tape at any tempo you wish. Greater accuracy and faster lock up, especially on systems that are integral to your music sequencing software.

A drawback is that a stand alone unit has to have tempo changes and time signature changes programmed into it, not the sequencer which is then triggered by MIDI clock. However dedicated SMPTE units like C-Lab Notator's Unitor are much more sympathetic to the software.

In contrast, sequencer generated MTC can contain tempo and time signature change information which the sequencer can follow on playback, so no reprogramming is necessary.

❏ Which track for recording time code?

The edge track is the best because that will minimise any crosstalk from the abrasive time code. Many multitracks like the Tascam series assume you are going to use the edge track (track 8 on an eight track machine for example) and allow you to alter level and switch off the noise reduction on that track.

On narrow track formats like quarter inch eight track you must be careful to avoid crushing the edge tracks by poor storage – it could cause drop out on the time code track.

❏ What level?

Use the manufacturer's recommended level or experiment until you find the lowest level at which the unit will retrieve the code. I usually record code at –7 to –10dB. On a digital machine crosstalk is not an issue.

❏ The desk

If you run the code through the desk to alter its level when you are first striping the tape that's OK as long as there is no program material being recorded at the same time, but the approved method of recording is to take the signal straight to the tape machine. Never run the tape back to the synchroniser via the desk unless you want to check its integrity. Such is the nature of the sound that it will crosstalk on channels and you will end up with a nice bit of time code in the background of your mix.

❑ Noise reduction

dbx can sometimes cause problems because of its compression and pre emphasis on encode and expansion on decode. The encoded signal may well saturate the tape – again due to its abrasive nature, and the reader may have problems with level fluctuation on replay.

Other NR systems seem to be able to cope, and to be honest so does dbx nine times out of ten. However, most machines with dbx now allow you to switch it out on the time code track.

❑ Adjacent tracks

On analogue machines, transient (fast attack, short duration) sounds like drums can crosstalk to the code track and fool the unit reading the code that this is a pulse. Consequently the reader will crash or gradually drift out of synchronisation. So on the adjacent track it's a good idea to use soft attack sounds that are not going to be high in the mix, and then you won't hear any time code crosstalk coming back!

❑ Recording with time code

A good sequencer will give you several options when recording, including real time and step time, in MIDI data, drum style grid or notation form. You tend to find the one that suits you and stick to it. But how does this recording method fit in with the rest of your system?

❑ Starting with the groove

Most musicians seem to forget tape synchronisation until the main body of the song has been performed and arranged entirely using the sequencer. A typical scenario in pop, rock and dance production would first involve establishing a groove by recording drum parts into the sequencer's memory and using these to trigger the voices in a sound module like a drum machine or sampler. Or by sampling a breakbeat, finding the best loop point and tempo then embellishing with other drum voices.

Adding a simple bass line and chord progression will then allow you to establish the arrangement outline for a song whether you have written the melody or not, and at this stage in the writing process the ability to alter anything like key, tempo and form is a big plus.

Unlike using a conventional multitrack, you are free to experiment with variations, and when you've found the right arrangement embellish the individual sections with extra rhythmic or melodic parts. Tape synchronisation and vocals will follow, although in dance production the vocal may already be recorded into a sampler by this stage!

❑ Sync soon

For conventional vocals it makes sense to get the multitrack synchronised to the sequencer as soon as an arrangement and rough chords are down so you can put a guide vocal on tape. Many good musical ideas are inspired by the vocal melody, and you can also make absolutely sure that the key of the song is right.

❑ Performance first

Another method which is far less reliant on the sequencer and more on the player is to record time code then work on tempo and lay down a click track. The performer can then record chords and guide vocal onto the conventional multitrack for the track to be built around. This relies on a good link between the multitrack and sequencer as there will be far more tape shuttling using this method as you build up the track. A sequencer with MMC control of the tape machine would be an asset in this scenario but not a necessity.

❑ SMPTE trigger

You don't have to let the sequencer dictate your working method because there are devices that allow you to establish a tempo related synchronisation code towards the end of the session. A trigger to SMPTE, MTC or MIDI clock convertor with tempo mapping is necessary. This will convert an audio pulse like a bass drum, or better still a click track into time code which follows the tempo changes of a real player.

In practice it is easier to tap along and provide a pulse that way than rely on an audio trigger like a kick drum.

❑ Memory

Continuous controllers like aftertouch, pitch bend and modulation use up a lot of memory and while it's pretty obvious when you use the last two, aftertouch information will be sent out every time a key is depressed and so is less easily spotted. Users of sequencers with small memories are recommended to filter these out.

Even on more powerful computer based sequencers this information tends to get filtered off the edit screen as so much data makes editing confusing.

❑ Back it up

Remember to back up your information regularly and make a copy of your music software.

❏ **Sequencer delay feature**

Sadly not found on all sequencers but incredibly useful in the studio.
Apart from curing the MIDI delays of some sound modules you can use
this feature as a creative tool.

○ *PROJECT*

MIDI delay

Record a chord on track one, MIDI channel one, beat one at 120bpm.
Copy it three times to tracks two, three, and four. Delay track two by
125ms, track three by 250ms and track four by 500ms. Play the
sequencer and you will hear a delay effect. To make it more realistic
gradually reduce the velocity values of the chord on tracks two, three
and four progressively. Now the chord appears to have a decay tail.

Experiment by giving each repeat a different MIDI channel and sound.
You can also reverse this by moving the chord to bar two, beat one and
pre delaying the other tracks progressively 500ms, 250ms and 125 ms.

❏ **Triggered samples**

Something that's done a lot in studios is the triggering of samples to
replace or add to real drum voices. An audio signal is sent to a trigger-
MIDI unit from a snare drum for instance, and this is converted into a
MIDI note with velocity and channel information. Invariably an audible

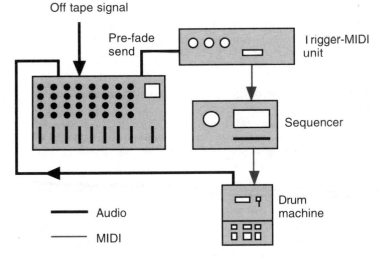

Triggering a drum voice from an off-tape signal via the desk

time delay occurs between the actual sound sent to the trigger-MIDI unit and the final sound, whether triggered on a drum module or sampler. If this MIDI information is recorded onto a sequencer synchronised to tape you can then pre delay the note triggers by the necessary amount to bring the sounds back into time.

Remember to disable the trigger unit once you have recorded your triggers into the sequencer otherwise you will get a through trigger as well as a recorded one. The time delay is usually in the region of 10 to 20ms.

❏ Timing

If you don't have fancy quantise functions, delays can alter the rhythmic feel of a piece. A snare drum in a ballad would undoubtedly be played late to the beat by a real drummer yet a quantised snare drum will be too much on top of the beat in a sequencer. Using the delay function could 'humanise' that snare.

❏ Transpose

Changing the key of a track, a section of a song, or even a whole song may be desirable, and a sequencer can do this automatically without you having to play it again in another key in semitone steps. Remember to disable transpose on the drum tracks because it will upset your drum mapping.

❏ Fatten up the bass

Some bass synthesiser sounds are better when you put in the octave below by copying the original to another track and transposing it. In this state the lower register can contain too much bass but a useful trick is to reduce the velocity value of the copy until it sounds right.

❏ Velocity, compression and quantisation

Velocity values are often used as crude level controls while a piece of music is being built up, but remember that this could affect the sound being triggered if it has been programmed to alter with a higher velocity value. Compression is similar to the rack mount sort in that it averages the level and as such is a useful tool when a piece has been badly played. However, like the real thing it can take all the dynamics out of a performance if overused.

With so many types of quantisation available on the larger sequencers, the term 'musical straight jacket' is no longer a justifiable criticism. However many basic sequencers and drum machines have only limited parameters, and it really is worth trying to play something into the sequencer in real time without quantisation if possible.

❑ A quantised drum part with feel

To make a solid drum part with some feel, quantise the kick and snare but play the hi-hats in real time. If you loop them give it a couple of bars so there is some change in accenting. Better still, record real hi-hats!

○ *PROJECT*

Using program change messages

These can be recorded into your sequencer in step time or real time and then used to recall patches on your outboard, sound modules and desk mutes during the mix. This is especially useful if you have a limited set up but wish to take advantage of different sounds and effects as the mix runs.

○ *PROJECT*

1: Start of song

Leave one or two bars (these could even be your count in) at the start of the mix and put program and control change commands into the sequencer to recall the effects and sounds you need for the song. Store this to disk with your music and all your sounds will be ready whenever you roll the song.

○ *PROJECT*

2: On the fly

Change patches on sound modules and effects as the song is running by inserting program changes at appropriate places in the song.

❑ Get the timing right

Slightly offset the program change command before the beat at which you want it to change because some synthesisers and outboard take a fraction of a second to load the new program and this delay is audible.

❑ Program change of multi-effects units

Two effects units are usually enough. One is left on a general reverb setting and the other used as a 'floating' unit for special effects – different delay times or a longer reverb in places. This can be given program change messages at suitable times in the mix.

❏ Better late than early

If changing long reverbs and delays to a different program make sure that you do not cut off the decay tail by sending a program change too early. Also if the change is a little tight you can get away with it by changing the patch on the beat that the music changes and it will not be so noticeable.

❏ MIDI program numbers

You may have noticed that program numbers do not always correspond between different manufacturers and some program change mapping either on the sequencer or target equipment may be necessary.

❏ Using controllers in the studio

Controller messages can be used to edit parameters on outboard as well as synthesisers where the manufacturer allows for such control. In such situations you will have to decide which controller you want to use (a modulation wheel on a synthesiser for instance) and a target parameter on the outboard which will respond to the information being sent, such as reverberation decay time. A glance at the MIDI implementation chart of the equipment will tell you what it's capable of.

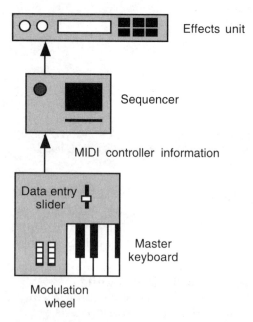

Effects unit

Sequencer

MIDI controller information

Data entry slider

Master keyboard

Modulation wheel

Recording MIDI control change messages to alter effects parameters

❏ Use the mod wheel

Controller information, like program change commands can be recorded into a sequencer in real time or step time for changes as the mix is running. However as there is so much information in control change data it is far less time consuming to record in real time using a modulation wheel or data fader. This information can then be reassigned on the sequencer to the controller number of your choice or mapped at the unit which will receive it. Be careful not to fill up the memory of a small sequencer by using too much control data.

Commonly found controllers are:

Modulation wheel	1	Data entry	6
Breath control	2	Volume	7

In addition, a good master MIDI keyboard will allow you to assign controller numbers of your choice to sliders on the main panel.

○ PROJECT

Reverb

Change the decay time as the track is rolling for a single sound strike when you have a gap or the space in the mix to hear the effect. Shortening the decay increases tension – lengthening the decay gives a panoramic, spacious effect. Try lengthening the decay on long sustained notes whether instrumental or sung. A similar effect can be produced with echo if you shorten or lengthen the decay time.

❏ Using the pitch change controller

If you assign the controller to the fine pitch or coarse pitch parameters you can use it for many effects. For example on pitch changers that are not intelligent you can use it to change the pitch to that of a musical harmony rather than a fixed interval. Try it on a drum hit, dropping the pitch slightly as the drum is struck to give the impression that the pitch of the drum is also changing. Slight, random pitch changes on snare hits will make a drum machine sound more like a real player.

○ PROJECT

MIDI EQ

Create a dynamic filter sweep by assigning the controller to a frequency band and altering it on a narrow Q setting. This is great for looped sequences and wah wah effects.

❑ Volume (controller 7)

One of the most useful controllers it is frequently incorporated into sequencer software as a MIDI mixing page. Ideal for level changes and mutes you can sit back as the mix takes place and lend an objective ear!

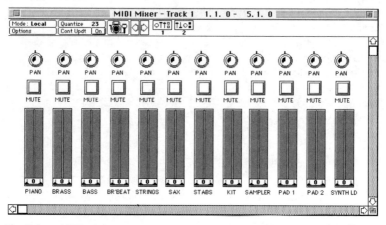

The Cubase MIDI mixer page

❑ Pan (controller 10)

Again useful in the mix for stereo placement or more adventurous auto panning of repetitive sequences.

❑ System exclusive

A glance at the back pages of most manuals is enough to put you off system exclusive messages for life. However you may already be using them for data storage and retrieval and for editing if you have software that allows you to edit and categorise your sounds.

❑ Data storage and retrieval

In the studio you could be flying sounds into the keyboard via system exclusive information as the track is running. This is not as complicated as it seems because many sound modules allow you to dump sounds individually – a relatively small amount of information which will not upset the running of the sequencer when retrieved. This is really useful only if the patches have been altered in a sound module since you last worked on the composition. At least you know that the correct ones will be transmitted for the song every time.

Apart from the pose value of this, it is however more practical to do a system exclusive dump of the entire program memory or multi timbral set up you are using, recording it within the first few bars of the sequence. This ensures that every time you load the song you have the correct patches at your disposal.

❑ Avoid loops

If your system exclusive dump is not a two way communication then it is advisable to make sure that a loop does not occur when recording the data to the sequencer. Use a filter on the output, switch off the MIDI thru or as a last resort unplug the MIDI In lead to the sound module.

❑ Editing

Some sequencers have the ability to edit the parameters on sound modules, and this can be useful on the fly in a mix as well as for more standard editing purposes. This method has certain advantages over editing the sound on the synthesiser module itself. To start with it allows you to have access on a larger screen, secondly it allows you to alter more than one parameter at a time.

Recording this information could be as simple as you changing it on the module with the sequencer in record, or more complex – involving a learning process for the sequencer which can then assign the parameters to faders. Parameters that are most effectively altered on the fly are the filter and obvious envelope ones like attack.

❑ Store it!

Remember that once stored to disk all this information can be recalled for your mix when you load the sequencer.

❑ MIDI machine control (MMC)

Only computer based sequencers are liable to use MMC – a part of MIDI that allows you to operate the tape machine from the sequencer. The obvious advantage is that you can control your whole recording system from one place as all the multitrack transport, locate and record functions can be accessed on sequencing software that supports MMC. When you move the sequencer to bar 36 the recorder will follow to the correct position. However it does require a two way communication which will complicate your synchronisation system. You press play on the sequencer and a message is sent to the tape machine to start, timecode running on the tape machine is then picked up by the sequencer and the two begin to run together.

❏ MIDI muting

Many desks can now be fitted with MIDI muting which can be recorded to a sequencer in real time on the fly, in step time or in mute snapshots using an on-board memory of the desk mute status at a given point in time. The mutes are individually triggered by MIDI note number and velocity or controller information, and for those systems with on board memories these can be recalled with program change commands. It's actually easier to use an external sequencer to record the information and edit it because the screen is larger and the processing more powerful on a dedicated sequencer.

❏ Use channel 16 for desk info

Keep the desk information as far away from the other MIDI data as possible to avoid confusion – MIDI channel 16 is often used.

❏ Benefits of mute automation

- Mute up to start of song
- Channel close down at track end
- Individual channel mutes to eradicate noise
- Mutes act as noise gates for drums
- Effects send muting for special effects like single word echo
- Dub effects for remixes – dropping instrumentation in and out.
- Splitting channels and using muting to change between them for simple level, EQ or effect send changes
- Ability to save and recall this information when necessary
- Less manual moves on the mix – hence greater engineer objectivity

○ PROJECT

Set up some simple automation

In the unlikely event that you have some free effects units on the mix you can get simple automation of volume, EQ and mute without the benefit of a programmable console. The most simple example would be to route an off tape signal through a programmable effects unit en route to the desk. Provided you can turn off all the effects in the patch you then have two ways to control the signal:

1 MIDI program change

Set up a few patches with variable output levels and send sequencer program changes to the unit at appropriate times during a mix. If you don't have a sequencer you can still change the patches by foot switch.

2 MIDI controller messages

Map a continuous controller to the output level parameter of the effects unit. Record some level changes into a sequencer synchronised to tape and then play back.

❏ EQ and mute

Obviously you can apply the same method but adapt it for zero volume or EQ parameter control of the signal too. While you can effectively mute the signal going through an effects unit, let me remind you that the console channel actually remains open and could be a source of noise if the gains are high or if there is HF equalisation.

○ PROJECT

Volume automation using a noise gate

Triggering the gate via the key input can give two preset levels. Feed the audio off tape signal into the normal gate input and take the output to the console on the appropriate channel insert point.

Setting the high level With the gate open, set the level you want to hear the signal at on the channel fader for the loud passages. Next decide where you want these to occur and record a sine wave style synthesiser tone into the sequencer for the duration of these passages. The output of the synthesiser on playback is fed to the key input of the noise gate (now in external trigger mode) and will fully open the gate for these sections.

Setting the low level For the quiet sections, the range control can be adjusted to give the amount of decibel drop you require. Now whenever the gate is triggered you will get your increase in volume, and when the trigger is absent the volume will fall to the level of the range control in dB. Attack and release controls on the gate can be used to smooth the transition.

Likewise a compressor can be activated from its side chain input to alter the level of a signal. An increase in volume from the trigger tone will result in a volume decrease for the signal running through the unit, and you have a basic level control!

13 How do I get a good mix?

❑ What is a good mix?

A good mix is one that communicates the mood of the composer, a marriage if you like between the quality of the recorded performance and the technical skill of the production team. Most of you reading this book will be taking on both roles, so your main problem is going to be lack of objectivity. It's an idea to get someone you trust to lend an unbiased ear to the mix!

Chapter 3 on arranging and track layering stressed the importance of getting the right sounds to tape, and you will reap the benefits of this at the mix stage: less or no equalisation, clarity, all the instruments occupying a useful place in the mix, little level changing, basic and effective use of effects.

❑ Reaching the mix

You could have arrived at this point a number of ways – there is no standard approach. As you build up the track during overdubbing by working on the main faders instead of the monitor section, you can get rough levels, basic equalisation and choice of effects sorted as you build up the song. Once you reach a position where you have finished overdubbing and want to mix, it then becomes a fine tuning process.

In another scenario you may be mixing the track with a clean slate by switching from off tape listening on the monitor section to the main channels, or simply by mixing some days after the recording was finished and the desk used for something else. Whatever the case it is a good idea to have a break between the overdubbing and mixing stage, even if it's just overnight. The things that you thought were working after a long session can sometimes be exposed as mistakes in the cold light of day.

A rough mix on cassette or DAT can help you remember your original intentions if there is a considerable gap between overdubbing and mixing.

❑ Starting the mix

When mixing from scratch make sure that unwanted desk channels and auxiliary sends are switched off and equalisation flat, although it's a good idea to have some effects patched in and ready to use. At this point you can set up the channel input gains for monitoring off tape and mark up the desk with a chinagraph pencil as you do so. Once this is done switch from PFL to solo in place mode, if you have one, as this is much more useful for listening to comparative levels during the mix. Set your master faders to zero dB and you're ready to begin.

❏ Tips on monitoring

Get a reference! You need to get used to your monitoring system if you want to achieve good results. Play music you know well through the speakers as a reference, especially to check treble and bass. It also helps to play music with a similar sort of production sound or style if that is what you are aiming for on the mix – everybody does it!

❏ Low frequencies

The main thing to watch is overcompensation for bass on small speakers which cannot possibly give you a true representation of the LF end of the mix. Here familiarity with the speakers is paramount, but if you are still not sure apply some sort of bass filter on the overall mix around 50Hz to gradually roll off the bass end.

❏ Monitor position and room acoustic

While this is a big subject, some useful pointers are not to use speakers that are too large for the room or position them in the corner, make sure that you have no audible reverberation or high frequency reflections in the area where the speakers are positioned – i.e. make sure that the room is not too live at this point. For stereo clarity, sit equidistant from the speakers with the tweeters rather than the drivers pointing towards your ears.

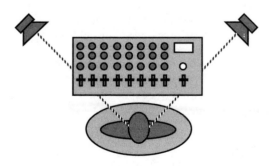

Nearfield monitoring position and soundfield

❏ Levels

What level should you mix at? The simple answer is at the level it's intended to be played at. This may not be feasible for dance projects in a domestic setting, so try to hear the mix over a large system in a club if possible. For most other projects if you are used to your speakers you can monitor at a reasonable level most of the time, but check the mix when both loud and quiet (can you still hear everything?) before consigning it to tape. Also remember that prolonged listening to loud music will alter your sense of treble and eventually lead to hearing damage.

❏ Finding basic levels – the rhythm method

You could start with the rhythm section, getting a rough balance between drums, bass and main chordal instruments before moving on to vocals and melody instruments. This is not a bad idea as once you've set these levels they rarely need to be altered again while the mix is running. However be careful to leave a gap in the audio sound field for the vocals – it's tempting to work for too long on the backing at this stage and make it fill the mix.

❏ Vocals first

Another method involves first dealing with what you consider to be the most important element of the mix – vocals for example – and mixing everything to that.

This has the advantage of making sure that nothing obscures what you most want to hear and that the instrumentation is sympathetic to the vocals.

❏ Marking it down

A chinagraph pencil is useful for marking the fader channels when you have found the basic levels. A common fault is to start off with the fader levels too high and end up with an overloaded left/right bus and no headroom available on the channel faders for instruments that need to stand out. So establish a working level that allows you to leave the main faders at 0dB without overload. Returning to the channel faders it's quite usual for more than one position to be marked if you need to do any gain riding on a particular sound.

❏ No scribble strip?

Presumably you've got a track sheet by now, but if there's no scribble strip on the desk some masking tape can be used – this won't strip the paint off when you remove it! It's also useful if you're working on several mixes at a time to keep each strip of tape in case a remix is necessary.

❏ Pan positioning

Pan positions can be worked on as you're setting levels because they follow a logical course for the most part. With a band for example you could take the Bob Clearmountain approach and pan the different instruments to the positions they might occupy on stage. Notice that the vocalist is positioned centre stage but the central position is also occupied by the bass instruments and snare.

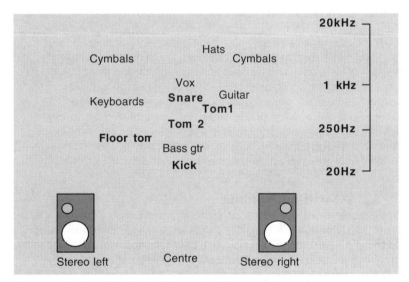

Stereo positioning of band mix with rough guide to main frequency areas of attention

None of these instruments conflicts with vocals in frequency range so clarity is maintained, but there are reasons why bass instruments are normally panned to the centre: On vinyl it is very difficult to cut such large sound waves to one side of the stereo. Low bass is omnidirectional and could be said to have a less defined stereo position. Obviously if you panned the bass hard left or right, as is possible in this age of digital recording, you will get an interesting, if unbalanced effect as the bass end of the mix carries most of the punch and energy.

Likewise the snare in most recordings is still mixed fairly loud and in stereo this will have an unbalanced effect if panned to one side with nothing to interact with it on the other side of the stereo.

○ **PROJECT**

Complementary panning

In contrast to the low frequency sounds, multiple high frequency signals are best panned because they may occupy the same frequency range and so lose clarity.

As an illustration of this, try panning a cabasa and hi-hat to the same place in the stereo then to opposite sides. The effect is not only a more distinct mix but a rhythmic interaction between the two sounds.

❑ **Equalisation**

Although it's satisfying to use very little equalisation on the mix when your overdubbing has been immaculate, it doesn't always turn out that way and some creative EQ may be necessary to improve separation.

Where you have a dense mix and little clarity you need to limit the area of the audio spectrum occupied by some instruments. For example an electric guitar could have some lower mid and bass frequencies cut by a few dBs to allow the bass guitar to cut through. Likewise the extremes of its high frequencies can be cut without taking away the character of the instrument – suddenly the vocals and cymbals become clearer. Both are examples of subtractive EQ .

❑ **EQ without soloing**

For extreme cases the actual instruments when isolated could sound a little odd after equalisation, but always try and work with the concept of the whole mix in mind. A common fault is to solo channels one at a time and try to make the instruments sound as good as possible without referencing back to the main mix. Treble boost is then usually added which makes the next sound you listen to a bit dull in contrast, so you then have to add some treble to that and so on until the entire mix sounds far too toppy!

Unless there's a problem like a peak frequency or bass rumble try and equalise the sound without soloing it, then if it starts to clash you will hear it straight away. EQ cut buttons are a useful feature to check whether you've improved a sound or made it worse! Where all the sounds are a little dull it's better to use an EQ like a graphic or enhancer on the entire mix rather than add EQ to all the individual channels.

❑ **Leave it out!**

As you establish working levels for the mix and even after pan and equalisation, you could still find that it's too busy in some sections.

This is the point at which you prioritise what is important for the overall mix, even if it means eliminating the part you spent ages on!

The bottom line is to keep the parts that sound and interact best with the rest of the parts at that point in the mix. You can always use the lost instrument in an alternative mix.

❏ Effects

Pan and equalisation are not the only things that can improve separation. Delay effects can give a sense of depth and width to an instrument that will give it a place in the mix. The basic rule is that all effects should be treated with the same care and attention as an instrument when it comes to their impact on the overall sound.

❏ How many effects?

You might think that having a lot of effects will enable you to get a better mix but it 's the choice of effect that's important and you may be surprised at how few are actually used. Using too many – e.g. different sort of reverb for every instrument – is confusing for the ear and results in a quite unnatural sound – as if the musicians are all playing in different rooms. Likewise too much echo and modulation can muddy the entire sound. So if you want a specific large effect, then there must be space in the mix for it. Some of the most interesting mixes have a sparse instrumentation where there is plenty of room to hear the effects.

❏ Reverb

Imagine your mix as a soundscape that has width (pan), height (equalisation) and depth (delay effects). All these can be affected by use of reverb, so it must be carefully chosen. One general reverb is sufficient for the instrumentation with another for vocals and special effects.

❏ General reverb

A simple rule can be applied here. For up-tempo tracks a faster reverb decay time is best and for slow tracks a longer decay time. The reasoning is simple, if for example you apply a long reverb to drums at a fast tempo the reverb will still be decaying from the first snare trigger as the next snare is hit. Consequently you will lose clarity as the reverbs overlap and some phasing may also occur to exacerbate the problem!

Some sounds need more reverb than others – they can't all have the same amount or your mix will sound as if it's being played from a distance! And remember that your channel aux sends are simple level mixers for the reverb input signal.

❏ **Reverb tip**

Room, short hall and gated reverbs are useful for up-tempo songs. Plate and hall with some pre delay and modulation for slow tracks. Dance mixes may have little or no reverb on the instruments.

❏ **Delay**

It's a good idea to have a range of delays available. The current fashion is to tempo match them to the speed of the track. If you know the bpm, convert it into millisecond delay times. If you don't, use a continuous instrument like a snare drum and send it to the delay, adjusting the time until the repeats fall into line with the snare strikes. You could also plug in a microphone and click your fingers to get the time.

❏ **Channels as effects returns**

It is important to be able to have fader control of the important effects returns to allow gain riding at crucial moments for performance mixes. It's also quicker and easier to equalise the effect on a main channel and have the ability to send the effect back to itself or to another effect, which dedicated effects returns don't always allow.

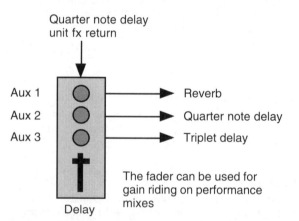

Quarter note delay
unit fx return

Aux 1 → Reverb
Aux 2 → Quarter note delay
Aux 3 → Triplet delay

Delay

The fader can be used for gain riding on performance mixes

If a channel is used as an effects return the engineer has many other creative options. In this example the delay effect signal can be sent to the reverb, to the triplet delay for a more complex echo effect, or even to itself for dub echo.

❏ **Two classic examples**

Dub echo effects are achieved by sending an echo back to itself until the repeats build up close to feedback and then cutting the send signal before it is out of control. Send a mono delay signal to a reverb for a really expansive sound.

❏ Equalisation of reverb and other effects

One major difference between expensive and budget effects is clarity. Budget reverbs for example tend to fill the mix and need far more EQ work to retain separation. Conversely effects can also be used to 'sit' instruments in the mix by adding frequencies that are missing or giving them extra dimensions of depth or width. Here are some common examples of how EQ can help

Vocal sibilance is emphasised by the high frequency bandwidths of modern effects, and lowering the bandwidth to 10 or 12kHz can often cure this problem. Cutting the really low frequencies on a vocal effect will get rid of rumble and spill as a vocal has no energy below about 100Hz. Instead of using equalisation to add presence to a sound try feeding it to a bright reverb. Rolling off the bass using a high pass filter on a general reverb will improve clarity on the bottom end of the mix.

❏ Compression

Even if you've compressed the signal to tape, compression is often added for vocals to keep them even during the mix, as they are usually mixed quite loud. Compressing analogue tape signals excessively will bring out the tape noise, so be careful.

❏ Compressing the entire mix

To smooth peaks apply some soft knee compression:

threshold	gain reduction on peaks only
attack	fast
release	0.5s
ratio	2:1 – 5:1

Sometimes when you apply an overall compression to a mix with a high vocal level the vocal ends up over compressed and the backing not enough. To avoid this sub group the backing and compress it independently of the vocal.

❏ Make your mix radio friendly

Some producers monitor their mixes through compressors set at the sort of levels you would expect from radio broadcasts to see if they are radio friendly, but do not actually compress the signal to the two track master. You would have to run a compressor in line with the monitor output and not the left/right bus to do this. Broadcast compression ratios are generally a pretty extreme 10:1+.

❑ Noise in the mix

Overdriven guitar is the usual culprit but the solution can be applied to any noisy sound. Use an expander gate if possible because it tracks the signal all the time, following the attack and decay characteristics of the instrument. It is therefore more subtle than the switch action gate where noise is audible as soon as the gate is opened.

❑ Cleaning up spill on drums

A switch action noise gate like the Drawmer DS 201 is excellent for this, but my advice is to gate drums only if they really need it. The worst culprit is always the snare drum where hi-hat spill can affect both how you equalise the snare channel and whether you can send the signal to the reverb. In the latter case the continuous signal of the hi-hat re-triggers the reverb causing a wash of sound that loses mix clarity.

Here are my suggested snare gate settings:

HPF	300 – 500Hz	attack	fast
LPF	1kHz	hold	200ms
		release	50ms+

In the case of extreme spill where a gate affects the snare sound too much, split the channel as described below in the section 'channel splitting – triggers'.

❑ Using effects on the entire mix

All the methods described in Chapter 14 can actually be applied on the mix if you are confident enough to commit them to the master tape at this stage. Effects would be connected to the left/right insert points.

❑ Gain riding

In most cases, once you have found the fader, pan, equalisation and effects levels for the majority of instruments, you are left with only one or two that need some manual adjustment on the mix. By making several passes through these sections you can find the levels the faders need to be moved to and mark them with a chinagraph pencil. It really pays to practice moving the faders and getting used to the difference in level this actually makes for the sound around the critical –5dB to +5dB region, where most gain riding is done.

If you end up gain riding a channel throughout the mix you should seriously think about using a compressor to even out the level provided it does not compromise the sound.

❏ Performance mix

Production dynamics can be made quite exciting by manual operation of the mix – changing channels, adding effects and gain riding effects return faders. This kind of mixing becomes more like a performance and is impossible to recreate on each pass. However, you can edit all the best bits together in post production.

❏ Channel splitting

What happens when you have too many manual operations to do at critical points in the mix? Before upgrading to automation or inviting the band to join in on fader management, see if a little channel splitting will do the trick. It helps if you have a patchbay with half normalisation on the inserts for this but there are other methods of splitting a signal from the desk, such as using a pre-fade send.

    The method involves taking the insert send from the patchbay of the channel that you want to adjust and plugging it into a free channel line input. This effectively gives you two channels (referred to as channels A and B) with the same sound on them which can be used for level, equalisation and effects control – or a combination of all three.

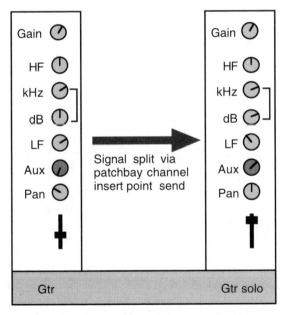

Split channel demonstrating change in level, EQ, pan position and effect send gain for guitar solo

The four following tips are achieved with the help of channel splitting.

1 Level adjustment

Preset channel A at the normal level and B at the level you want it to change to. Mute A and open B when you want this level change to occur, and reverse when you want to return to the original level. This is ideal for solos or where there is track sharing on the multitrack and the tape levels are incorrect.

2 A change of equalisation

A sound may need to be altered as the mix is running to suit the other instruments in different sections of the song. For example the muted guitar of the verse needs to be more brash in the chorus. You could in this example give the guitar on channel B more upper mid or HF equalisation and simply switch it in and out for the chorus.

3 Different effects

Similarly the instrument may require more reverb or delay at certain points in the mix. Rather than reach up to alter the effects send and possibly also the return, channel B could be preset with a higher aux send value. This allows you to make the change quickly and effectively.

4 Triggers

There may be occasions where you want to trigger an effect or a sampler by isolating the sound being used as the trigger. For example a snare drum on a real drum kit being sent to a reverb will also have hi-hat spill that will trigger the reverb and result in a wash of sound.

For clarity you can gate the snare channel so that the reverb is only triggered by the snare but this can often have an adverse effect on the snare sound itself. Triggering the reverb from a gated snare running on channel B while leaving the channel A snare open will solve the problem. However now you have two dry snares, an open and a gated one. To mute the gated channel B snare without losing the effects send signal, simply turn off the left/right routing and leave the fader in place.

❏ Setting master record levels

When you are establishing the two-track record levels, always look for the peak signal on the track to set up your maximum record level. If this is way above the average signal level of the entire track then you should consider whether you need to alter the mix or the level of the peak instrument(s) to achieve a higher average signal. The most punchy mixes vary very little between peak and average and this also allows you to get a good signal to noise ratio for analogue recording with no noise reduction.

For DAT recording, although the dynamic range is greater and the tape itself noise-free in theory, the higher the level the better the quality. For budget DATs this certainly holds true for acoustic music where there is a greater dynamic range than rock and pop. However you now have a quandary – the levels need to be high but you don't appear to have much headroom for peaks.

A compressor will help here, but try not to compromise the sound by over squashing the dynamics. As a failsafe a limiter can be set to operate at –2 or 3dB below zero to avoid any overload.

Suggested limiter settings:

attack	fast
threshold	for signals rising above -3dB on the DAT (can be calibrated using a tone).
ratio	20:1
release	0.5s

❑ Playback

It's quite normal practice to check out mixes on all sorts of systems to make sure that the mix doesn't just sound good on the the one you mixed it on. The car stereo is a favourite for many as it is the place they listen to most of their music. For others it is ghetto blasters or Walkmans. An oft quoted favourite which I can vouch for is the 'listening from another room' test. If it still sounds good then you've cracked it.

14 Post production tips

Many people assume that once you've done the mixing that's the end of the matter. But for a serious project like a cassette, album or CD a lot more remains to be done.

Compiling the right tracks in the right order with the right length gaps is just part of the story. You may need to do some editing, control peak signals with compression and even add EQ for the sake of sound continuity if the project has been recorded using different equipment over a long period of time. Individual track levels are also likely to vary and you may have recorded some mixes at different sampling rates to others. All are part of the process of post production.

❑ Deciding on the running order

The track running order and final length of the production master are usually the first considerations. Here you must decide which mixes you are going to use and whether they are going to need any audio sweetening. First you need to time the running length of each individual track and assume something like a four second gap between them. For cassette based projects, this actually dictates your track order more than you might think, if you want each side to be roughly the same length! Once you've done this run all the tracks onto cassette in the correct order, live with it for a few days and see if they work.

❑ Things to avoid

- Putting two tracks with the same musical key and rhythmic feel side by side. They could have more impact in a different positions.
- Having too many tracks with long-winded introductions
- Big changes in level or equalisation from one track to another
- Long gaps
- Noise between tracks like hiss or earth loops
- Bad fades
- Using a weak track for the opening of a tape or CD

On this last subject, your first track must have impact, but it does not necessarily have to be up-tempo. It should be a mood setter, a track that encapsulates what the band or project is all about.

❑ Gaps

The interval of silence between tracks is not just the bit where there's no music, it has an important atmospheric role itself. After the most amazing track you've ever heard in your life you need a little space to contemplate how brilliant it was, and another couple of seconds gap will allow you to do it justice!

When moving from a moody downbeat number to an up-tempo rocker, a gap of only two seconds is going to be something of a shock! After all, remember that music is trying to create mood and convey emotion. On the other hand if your intention is to surprise and create rapid mood swings then you can buck convention and use gaps to your advantage.

Finally, bear in mind that long fades can often be misconstrued as very long gaps if you leave the standard four seconds between the end of the fade and the start of the following track. A gap of two seconds often works in such a case because the tail end of the fade can't be heard unless the music is being played really loud!

❑ Compiling the production master

Whether you're using an analogue reel to reel, DAT, digital editing software or humble cassette to compile the production master, some audio transfer has to take place. If there is no audio sweetening then a direct connection between one machine and another is the simplest option. Let's consider the two most common options.

❑ Reel to reel transfer

Pros:
- Gaps: easy to get the right gaps by calculating the length of the splicing tape against the running speed.
- Noise: by using leader tape you can virtually eliminate unwanted noise in the gaps.
- NR: you can use noise reduction if necessary but must use it on every track in a compilation.
- Levels: most machines have an input level so you do not have to use an external level control.
- Tape: you can use the side effects of analogue tape – compression, saturation, warm bass end to your advantage.
- Editing: arrangements can be altered and different mixes spliced together with practice.

Cons:
- Transfer: second generation with small loss in quality.

- Noise: analogue tape is a noisy storage medium, especially for acoustic music and compositions with a variable dynamic range.
- NR: good noise reduction systems are expensive and there may be unwanted side effects.
- Compatibility: a cassette copying facility will have to have a machine with the same noise reduction, EQ (NAB or IEC), tape speed and width functions as your machine to play your tape.
- Tones: generated from a decent sine wave generator are needed to ensure that the machine at the other end will be lined up the same way as yours.
- Editing: is destructive and if a mistake is made you may damage the master irretrievably.

❑ DAT to DAT transfer

Pros:
- Transfer: digital transfer using digital i/o will give no loss in quality. Analogue transfer will give very little change.
- Noise: no tape noise floor to consider.
- NR : no noise reduction system required.
- Compatibility: no alignment considerations.
- Levels: greater dynamic range.
- Tape: cheaper, longer running time on DAT tape, less physical storage space needed.

Cons:
- Gaps: hard to get accurate gap lengths.
- Noise: hard to eliminate noise in the gaps unless some noise reduction is used between DAT machines.
- Levels: theoretically DAT needs a higher consistent level to sound best, but this can be a problem with material that has a wide dynamic range. Compression may be needed to solve this.
- Incompatibility: between sample rates of 44.1kHz and 48kHz. A convertor may be needed.
- Some portable DAT machines (Teac and Casio) use pre-emphasis (a kind of treble boost encoded on recording and decoded on playback) to give a measure of noise reduction. Some editing software does not recognise and decode this in the digital domain which can lead to tapes that sound thin, toppy and noisy.
- Editing: can't be done on a DAT machine.
- Copy prohibit: some machines encode information to tape which will allow only one digital copy to be made of the tape. A copy prohibit stripper will be needed if you intend to make multiple copies.

❑ Some problems solved

A fairly accurate gap can be achieved when DAT to DAT copying if you record the track allowing the recording DAT to run on and put down time code for about ten seconds after you have stopped the playback DAT. Continuity of time code is important because some DAT machines will not play past a point where code is missing and also your ID numbers will be innaccurate.

Line the the next track up on the playback DAT about two seconds before the music starts and rewind the record DAT to a point two seconds before you want the music to start, that is, one or two seconds after the end of the last track.

Some DAT machines actually rewind the tape by two seconds when you record/pause and this must be taken into your calculations if you want to avoid chopping off the end of the preceding track when you hit record/play! If you press play on both machines together you will end up with a gap that is of an acceptable length, although I will be the first to admit that this method is a bit hit and miss! Check that you still have both the start and end of the tracks immediately after you have recorded them because it is very difficult to repair an erased section later.

❑ Digital editing of your master

A simpler option, to compile music that has been recorded to DAT, is to go to a digital editing suite, where any problems can be dealt with speedily in the digital domain. Even though the cost of this facility has dropped enormously the equipment itself is still out of the price range of most, and the hourly rate only worthy of the most important projects. I would heartily recommend it for a CD production but most cassette based projects will not be worth the expense.

❑ Use the same sample rate

If you decide that the project is worth it then you must make sure that all the tracks have been recorded at the same sample rate. 44.1kHz is best for CD projects, although any good facility should have a convertor for 48kHz masters. It also saves time and money if you present your material on one DAT tape in the right order, or as close to it as possible, because the music is run into and off the editor in real time (that's at least forty minutes each way, if it's straightforward, and this will be charged at the hourly rate).

❑ Adjusting levels

One song where levels are consistently hovering around 0db can sound much louder than another where the occasional peaks are high but the majority of the signal is much lower. Two ways to solve this are:

1. By aurally balancing the levels. To do this accurately you need to balance the rest against the one that sounds the loudest – using it as the reference.
2. By compressing the signal, provided it does not compromise the sound.

You may have looked at the levels on commercially recorded cassettes and wondered why they are consistently high and sound louder than your home recorded masters. The answer is that they have a limited dynamic range with a higher average signal.

❑ Subjective continuity

Listen to the way one track ends and plays into the next. Although it is the best idea theoretically to go for a consistently high level when you are cutting a CD, it does not always sound right subjectively. For example if a ballad is at the same level as the heavier track which follows it, the rocker will lose some of its impact unless you drop the level of the ballad fractionally. Such a change will not audibly compromise the quality of the recording but it will improve the listening experience.

❑ EQ'ing your master

Discrepancies in tone often occur in mixes which have been done at different times, and you must decide at the post production stage how you want the overall sound to be. This may involve running the mix through some equalisation to alter it during the compilation of the post production master.

You can easily use the desk equalisation for this by running the two track output through the line inputs of two channels on the desk and referencing against the tracks you think sound best. High quality outboard equalisation is a better choice, with graphics, parametrics, enhancers, and noise gate filters all proving useful. The following sections describe some typical problems and how to deal with them:

❑ Cutting out bass rumble

Use the desk EQ. If there is no bass filter use the bass shelving EQ and cut by a few decibels although this is usually too low (around 45Hz) to be totally effective.

Another very effective method of controlling rumble is to use the filter section on a noise gate if you have one. With the gate in stereo mode run the signal through the gate and switch it into key listen mode. This will allow you to use the filter section on the entire mix, leaving the treble alone and cutting the bass around 50–80Hz to suit. This is not as drastic as it may seem – remember that the filter has a slope and so does not actually cut everything dead below that frequency.

The filter section of a noise gate can be used to control unwanted bass rumble. If in use on a stereo signal remember to enable the stereo link switch.

For problem peaks in the bass end of a mix a frequency controlled compressor can work on just the bass with no phase problems. Establish the area you want it to work on (below 100Hz), and set the threshold, ratio, attack and release in the conventional manner.

If your compressor does not have built in equalisation, you can use a graphic or other equaliser connected to the side chain of the compressor to deal with the problem. Set the equalisation to operate in the bass area you want to be compressed most.

Some multi-effects units have equalisation but it is advisable to check the stereo integrity of their inputs and outputs. Also make sure that no signal degradation is taking place by switching the multi-effects unit into bypass mode to check.

❏ Adding presence

Use the desk EQ. Adding a slight boost at 10–12kHz using the sort of high frequency shelving equalisation found on most desks can usually sort this out. Watch out for any added noise which the HF boost will show up, particularly at the start, end and quiet sections of the track.

Stereo enhancers are often used for widening the mix as well as adding presence to a mix that lacks high frequencies. You need to be careful of the amount that you mix in, and take care when choosing the mid frequency from which you generate the higher ones.

Some of the basic models have a simple enhance mix control, whereas the more expensive may allow frequency band control of the audio enhancement. This could for example allow you to adjust the level of the bass in the mix.

❑ Using compressors and limiters

Where the mix has quite high signal peaks but a below average signal level, a compressor will come in very useful to bring the overall level up as well as cut the peaks. This can be run in line between the playback and the recording machine, but care must be taken to make sure that there is no unwanted noise brought out by the compressor at the start and end of tracks. Quite a lot of compressors now have built in expander gates to cope with just such a problem if it occurs.

Soft knee compression is more subtle, offering some compression all the time and making sure that there are no sudden dips in level on the signal peaks. The threshold should be set to give the required amount of gain reduction for the peaks, and the overall record level can then be increased on the mastering machine.

Although you should not be able to hear the compressor altering the sound of the piece, except for the apparent loudness, a glance at the meters should show a much more consistent reading. Some of the most punchy rock and pop mixes you may notice vary little more than 3dBs, whereas this will not really be acceptable for more traditional instruments.

If required, to get as high a signal as possible to DAT without overload, use the method described in the mixing section (in Chapter 13), which uses a limiter to prevent the signal rising above –2dB.

❑ Cleaning up with noise gates

Noise gates are particularly useful for cleaning up noise in the gaps and at song starts and ends when transferring from one DAT machine to another or from DAT to cassette.

With expander gates, the threshold setting is critical as the expander should only drop the level at moments when there is no signal present or as the signal decays. A high frequency filter which drops the bandwidth (and therefore the audible hiss) as the level gets lower can also be useful – handy for cleaning up fade outs where the ratio of signal to noise is bad. At the start of tracks where the expansion threshold level cannot remove enough of the noise without cutting the start of the music, the filter can also be employed and switched out when the main track is running.

Conventional noise gates are either on or off, which is fine for the start and end of tracks (provided the release works in tandem with the fade out), but not so useful within a track. You can however just switch it out for the bulk of the track or lower the threshold manually as the track is running to avoid any sudden disappearances as the level of the music falls below the gate threshold!

❏ Chaining gate, compressor and exciter

If you are chaining a gate and a compressor, the gate will normally run second in the chain. If you are using an exciter, put this after the gate so that it is not enhancing the levels of hiss!

❏ Adding reverb to the tail

Sometimes the tail end of a track has had the reverb cut too sharply in the mix or simply ends too suddenly. You can add some reverb to the tail end by putting the master through the desk and sending some of its signal to a reverb similar to the general one used on the mix. This can be added to the end of the mix by riding the effects return faders and fading the post mix on the main left right faders.

In a similar fashion other effects like dub echo or phase and flange may be added to the mix, but always monitor very carefully for any added noise and eliminate it.

❏ Adding other instruments

Likewise if you are otherwise satisfied with a mix but wish to add another instrument there is no reason why you can't run it onto the multitrack and add something, provided the signal degradation is not noticeable. Adding a small HF boost of around 2dB will counter this for analogue machines. On the mix use an appropriate effect like reverb to make the new instrument sit in the mix.

15   *Technospeak explained*

Active   Equipment that includes amplification electronics. For example an active guitar will contain a pre amplifier, and an active set of monitors will house the power amps in the speaker cabinets.

ADSR   Sound envelope attack, decay, sustain and release characteristics.

ADT   Artificial double tracking. Sound duplication using a short delay typically 35 – 60ms.

Aftertouch   Pressure sensitivity value of a MIDI instrument which can be assigned to performance characteristics like modulation, volume change and filter parameters.

Analogue   A signal as a continuously varying waveform. For example in analogue recording the signal is converted from sound wave to electrical voltage to magnetic energy and then back again.

Byte   A group of eight binary digits (bits).

Balanced   A balanced connection consists of two signals in reverse polarity but equal potential and isolated from an earth cable. Basically it provides a method of efficiently transferring a signal and eliminating noise at the same time. Used in most professional recording systems.

Bass proximity effect   Low frequencies accentuated by a pressure gradient microphone (eg. a dynamic) when used at close distance.

Bi-amping   This is found on the more expensive bass rigs and involves using a filter to split the bass and upper mid components of the sound to cabinets containing sympathetic speakers. Usually the bass to a 15 inch driver and the rest to a 2x10 inch cab.

Bounce   Process of mixing instruments already recorded to a free track. Often a way of combining tracks to free up more tracks if space is limited.

BPM   Beats per minute. A tempo reference.

Bussing   Process of routing a signal to its destination on a console. Using the LR switches or tape assign buttons to send the signal to the stereo mix or sub group faders would be two obvious examples.

Capacitor mic   A microphone that uses a charged lightweight plate as a moveable diaphragm separated from a fixed back plate by a small gap. As the diaphragm is moved by sound waves a change in capacitance occurs resulting in a current flow. Good quality electret mics work on a similar principle.

Cardioid   The heart shaped directivity pattern of most dynamic microphones.

Compansion   A noise reduction method that involves applying compression to a signal before recording and complementary expansion after.

Composite   The best sections from several takes mixed together to create one good take.

Compressor   Used to control varying levels in a signal, the compressor is an amplifier whose gain changes according to the level of the input signal.

Crosstalk   Breakthrough of signal on desk channels or adjacent tape tracks.

Cue   Communications route to artist, foldback and talkback.

dB   This unit expresses the ratio between two powers and considerably eases the equipment designer's mathematical burden. Literally a tenth of a bel.

DBX   Noise reduction system using pre-emphasis and de-emphasis in tandem with a compansion process.

De-essing   Process of reducing sibilance using frequency-sensitive compression.

DI   Direct injection. For example, a keyboard output connected directly to a desk line input.

Dolby   Noise reduction system based on frequency selective companding invented by Ray Dolby.

Driver   Large speaker in a monitor usually handling bass and lower mid frequencies.

Dry signal   Untreated signal.

Dynamic filter   A moveable equalisation filter that can create filter sweep effects, often found on multi-effects units.

Dynamic mic   A moving coil microphone where the diaphragm, with a coil of wire attached to it, is suspended in a magnetic field. Sound pressure waves cause it to move and an electromotive force is induced in the wire coil, thus giving a signal output.

EBU   European Broadcasting Union synchronisation standard. A frame rate of 25fps is used.

Enhancer   A processor that alters the tonal quality of the sound by creating new harmonics and subtle phase shifts.

Expander   A single ended noise reduction unit that reduces the level of a signal falling below a threshold by a preset ratio. Often a more subtle form of noise gating than the switching kind.

Foldback   Mix to the artist, usually using a pre-fade send.

Fundamental   The repetitive frequency by which we can determine the pitch of a note. It is usually the strongest in the waveform.

Frequency   The rate of repetition of a sound wave measured in cycles per second or hertz (HZ).

FSK   Frequency shift keying. A method of tape synchronisation.

Gain structure   Amplification stages within a desk, for example input gain, equalisation channel fader etc.,

Hard disk   Large amounts of digital information may be stored using this device. Typically used with computers it can store much more information than a floppy disk and provide quicker access to it.

Harmonics   Frequencies generated which are a multiple of the fundamental frequency.

HPF   High pass filter.

IEC   International Electrotechnical Commission – a standards organisation.

Impedance   In simple terms this is the resistance of a piece of electrical equipment to the flow of AC. It is measured in ohms and in practical terms is only a problem for the engineer when DI'ing passive electric instruments.

Insert point   Individual channel send /return connection.

Key listen   Switch on a noise gate that allows you to monitor the action of the filter section.

Legato   Slurring of notes – similar to the way a saxophonist might play.

Leslie effect   Cabinets with fixed speakers and rotating horns that were used with organ outputs to produce a Doppler style modulation. Modern effects can simulate this.

Limiting   A device for preventing overload by confining the volume of a signal below a preset level. A form of compression with severe gain reduction.

Matching transformer   A device which increases the power transferred when placed between two units of different impedances.

MIDI controller   Controllers are found on synthesisers as well as sequencers and can be used to alter MIDI parameters in real time. Volume, pan, modulation and pitch bend are just some of the more common controller functions.

MIDI implementation chart   An at a glance chart showing what a MIDI device is capable of within the MIDI specification.

MIDI loop   An information loop can be caused when the data from the MIDI output of a device is fed back to its MIDI input. The result is data error and in some circumstances, loss of full polyphony.

MIDI muting   Desk automation or on-board sequencing enabling desk channels or MIDI devices to be muted.

MMC   MIDI machine control. A part of the MIDI specification for control of tape machines.

Modulation   Control of one waveform by another

MTC   MIDI time code. SMPTE encoded for use in a MIDI system.

NAB   American standards organisation setting agreed frequency characteristics for tape.

Noise floor   Permanent level of noise present in a signal.

Normalisation   Method of wiring a patchbay so that sockets have permanently wired interconnections.

NR   Noise reduction

NTSC   National Television Standards Committee. On the TV broadcast standard of 525 lines the frame rate used is 30 drop frame (29.97 fps).

Ohm   Unit of electrical resistance or impedance.

Omni   An all around mic directivity characteristic.

Over-easy   Type of compression that is applied continuosly rather than threshold activated. Soft knee is the same.

Pad   An attenuation switch of typically -20dB found on the mic input gain of some desks.

Parametric   An EQ frequency shaper in which both frequency and bandwidth can be varied.

PFL   Pre fade listen. A feature that allows you to monitor the signal before it is faded up for recording or broadcast. Often used for setting up input gain levels.

Phantom power   Method of sending a dc supply to a capacitor microphone.

Phase   Position of a cycle that waveform has reached at a given point in time. When waveforms are out of phase their cyclic positions do not coincide.

Pizzicato   Plucked and damped note.

Polarity   Directivity pattern of a microphone.

Pre-delay   A delay time introduced before an effect occurs, for example, before reverb is triggered.

Pre-emphasis   Boosting the high signal component of a signal before recording. It is usually used with a de-emphasis on playback which restores the original signal but cuts tape noise.

Pre-production   Writing, programming and arranging work carried out prior to the main recording.

Program change   A MIDI channel voice message that will cause a patch to change on the receiving device.

PZM   Pressure zone microphone. It utilises the boundary effect – usually a floor or wall that it is attached to and picks up both direct and reflected sound simultaneously with a consistent frequency response.

Q   The symbol for the bandwidth control on a parametric equaliser.

Quantise   The ability to correct irregular notes' position and length.

RIAA   A record equalisation curve that minimises the effect of bass frequencies at high volumes when cutting vinyl. Turntables have RIAA outputs and need complementary inputs to a desk to work properly.

Sample rate   Rate at which digital samples are taken of a signal. A low sampling rate will result in poorer sound reproduction quality

Saturation   A magnetic tape is saturated when the output no longer increases with the input.

Sequencer   A system that can store, retrieve and manipulate MIDI data.

Slapback (delay)   Short delay, typically 60 – 150ms.

SMPTE   Society of Motion Picture and Television Engineers. Also a name given to a timecode running in real time – hrs, mins, secs and fps and has four frame rates – 24, 25, 30 and 30 drop.

Soft knee   (see Over easy)

Solo in place   Channel isolation where the level you hear corresponds to the level of the channel fader.

Speaker simulator   Characteristics of a speaker like HF reduction and mid-frequency sound colouration are emulated using this device.

SPL   Sound pressure level.

SPP   Song position pointers. Used for synchronisation, numbers are transmitted every six MIDI clocks which allow a slave device to chase and lock onto the nearest sixteenth note in a song being played by the master device.

Sweep mid   Mid frequency equalisation incorporating both gain and frequency controls.

Synchroniser   Device for linking the components of a recording system together using timecode.

System exclusive   MIDI messages which include a manufacturer's ID number and are typically used for quick storage and retrieval of data and to edit device parameters.

Threshold   Point above or below which an effect may operate.

Tie line   Connection between two points in a studio. For example between the control room and the playing area.

Timbre   Tonal characteristic of a sound.

Timecode   Code recorded onto a tape machine to enable it to be synchronised to other devices.

Trigger   Conversion of an audio input, for example a snare drum, to a MIDI note complete with channel and velocity information.

Unbalanced   Single signal connection surrounded by an earth lead. Used in most semi-pro studios.

Unidirectional   Directivity pattern of a microphone – sensitive to sound from one direction only.

Wet signal   A signal treated by an effect.

Watt   Unit of electrical power equal to one joule per second.

XLR   Type of plug used for balanced connections.